TEACHING TECHNIQUES

TEACHING TECHNIQUES

For Retarded and Pre-reading Students

By

MARY LOU DURBIN, M.A., Ed.S.

Special Services
Garden City, Michigan
Public Schools

With a Foreword by

Earl C. Kelley, Ph.D.

CHARLES C THOMAS • PUBLISHER
Springfield • Illinois • U.S.A.

Published and Distributed Throughout the World by

CHARLES C THOMAS • PUBLISHER

BANNERSTONE HOUSE

301-327 East Lawrence Avenue, Springfield, Illinois, U.S.A.

NATCHEZ PLANTATION HOUSE

735 North Atlantic Boulevard, Fort Lauderdale, Florida, U.S.A.

With **THOMAS BOOKS** *careful attention is given to all details of
manufacturing and design. It is the Publisher's desire to present books
that are satisfactory as to their physical qualities and artistic possibilities
and appropriate for their particular use.* **THOMAS BOOKS** *will be true
to those laws of quality that assure a good name and good will.*

Printed in the United States of America

A-2

To my parents,
Charles F. and Eunice Durbin

FOREWORD

Having read this volume, I am amazed at the many devices here set forth to be used with the handicapped, lately known as the disadvantaged. The book contains a veritable feast of materials and techniques. It should be of enormous help to the teacher who finds herself assigned to these groups.

The author is a person who is obviously filled with love and compassion for the little children entrusted to her care. Such people are the "salt of the earth" in all occupations, particularly so in teaching.

Except for a difference in materials and techniques, there is nothing here that would not be good for all children everywhere. What would be left would be attention to individual differences, which exist in all children, and feelings of affection and compassion for all. The expectation that all could learn the same things and profit by them would then have to be abandoned.

It is good that the less fortunate of our young have these techniques and materials, and that they have small enough classes to make attention to individual differences possible. I have sometimes wondered, in visiting an academic class, whether or not a child had to be born with or acquire handicaps to get a really good education.

I feel honored to have the opportunity to call attention to this book.

Earl C. Kelley, Ph.D.

PREFACE

Teaching Techniques for Retarded and Pre-Reading Students has been written to share instructional techniques and devices with teachers of pre-reading students in the regular classroom who are delayed in the readiness skills, teachers of primary retarded children and parents who can contribute much to their child's readiness for reading. There is planning to provide needed sequential skill development in selected learning areas and the possible prevention of some reading problems from later confronting insufficiently prepared readers who may have lacked a prolonged and reinforced readiness program preparatory to their introduction to formal reading.

An effort to achieve a clearly defined meaning of reading readiness and the skills involved has been effected. There is an emphasis upon the reading abilities for which certain readiness skills are necessary to prepare the child for successful reading. The teacher of pre-reading students who is aware of these readiness skills and their significance to reading success can plan definite instructional techniques and aims that are instrumental in developing the later reading ability for which the readiness skill is to prepare the child. The need for instruction through readiness to contain a preventive as well as a later remedial aim is very great.

Descriptions of devices and techniques suggested for utilization in activities to develop eye-hand coordination, visual perceptual skills and language abilities for the primary retarded child are included. Although the child development goals are alike for all children in the purpose of helping the child to grow in accordance with his potential and his individual needs, the goals differ in these ways: (a) the educable mentally retarded child needs much more repetition of instruction, reinforcement and review through a variety of interesting media; (b) the trainable retarded child needs to grow in vocabulary and communication skills, assume responsibility for his self-care needs to the best of his ability, learn to control hyperactivity and distractibility if possible to enable him to learn to complete simple tasks and follow directions; (c) the child who is delayed in the readiness skills needs instruction that is paced according to his readiness to acquire each skill and a prolonged readiness program to promote growth according to his individual needs, and (d) the disadvantaged child's greatest readiness need must be provided for during the early preschool years and requires opportunities for his experiential background, conceptual and vocabulary development, and his self-image.

A description of the various ways that audiovisual aids may be used in the introduction of the readiness skills emphasizes what skills are involved as well as the many audiovisual aids and materials that are available. The versatility of audiovisual aids provides for the possible application of many devices to stress one skill and enables the child to have needed review and repetition through interesting new activities.

The role of audiovisual aids in the readiness program is very important to the needs of the child who is delayed in the skills and must have a prolonged, varied and intensely interesting readiness background before his first approach to reading. Readiness skills, the audiovisual media, and the techniques, activities and ways of application for sequential skill development are described herein.

The section for parents of preschoolers includes a presentation of readiness skills and practical ways in which parents can help during the years that precede the readiness stage and during their child's pre-reading preparation. The author's summer school program involving preschoolers, their parents and prepared instructional materials and techniques contrived and devised from only the media and materials that parents would have available in the home or could easily obtain has been described.

Suggestions for some parents who wish to help their child in preparing for readiness instruction are given so that there may be an avoidance of a parental desire to give the child a too academic push before he is ready and the attitude of, "Whatever I do will probably be the wrong thing, so I'd better not do anything before he starts to school. They teach so differently today, anyway, so I don't know what to do."

The contents of the book are planned around the pupil needs, definite suggested materials and techniques to provide for them, and the involvement of parents in pre-reading activities for their children. The techniques and activities contained in this writing have been presented in activities with kindergarten children through the cooperation of their teacher, and have been evaluated in accordance with their apparent success with the children. Other sections contain the techniques for sequential skill development for mentally retarded children on the primary school level. It is hoped that this book will contain practical and helpful instructional aids for use by teachers and parents.

ACKNOWLEDGMENTS

THERE ARE MANY PEOPLE who deserve an expression of appreciation for their supportive help in the writing of this book.

The cooperation of Mrs. Opal Wagner, a teacher of kindergarten at Maplewood School in Garden City, Michigan, made possible the classroom activity and evaluation of the suggested instructional materials for use with pre-readers.

Mr. Glen Heavenridge, Memorial School administrator and the initiator and first director of the audiovisual program in Garden City, provided audiovisual aids for evaluative use with the mentally retarded children and other pre-readers. He offered helpful suggestions and sources for instructional materials for teacher use.

Mrs. James (Irene) Wood, the parent at whose home the summer school class for preschool children was held, also typed the manuscript. Her suggestions and encouragement have contributed greatly in this endeavor. She can brew a "powerful good" cup of coffee at the "threeish" or "fourish" hours of the morning!

My appreciation also is expressed to Doctor E. J. O'Leary, Superintendent of the Garden City, Michigan Public Schools, and Mr. John Giacomini, principal of the Maplewood School.

M.L.D.

Garden City, Michigan

CONTENTS

TEACHING TECHNIQUES

Chapter I

INTRODUCTION TO READINESS NEEDS

A CHILD'S READINESS enables him to proceed successfully and confidently from each skill level to the next as he derives pleasure and profit from reading. This ability to learn signifies a maturational level at which the pre-reader will be able to master the basic skills implicated in the presentation of formal reading instruction.

The child who is ready has previously become adept in many of these skills during his pre-school and kindergarten years, and is now eager to "get down to the brass tacks" of reading. He may be disappointed because he doesn't have the opportunity to begin reading the first day of school now that he is in first grade. Readiness for reading is very evident in the enthusiasm and interest shown by this child.

There are, however, many basic skills with which some children need more and prolonged assistance before they are ready to receive sufficient benefit from the readiness instruction in preparation for reading. These basic skills exist in all of the areas of reading readiness, and they vary according to the abilities and needs of the children. For these delayed learners, this requires help in getting ready for readiness. There seems to be a great need for a more prolonged emphasis, repetition of instruction and provision for additional time to permit these children to accomplish this growth. Their exposure to the formal reading program before they have achieved this level of readiness can only result in student failure, loss of self-confidence and dislike for reading later when it requires more complex skills and competencies.

Readiness preparation for these children demands more repetition of skill-building activities and a more varied and interesting reinforcement program. It is necessary for each skill level to be introduced in developmental sequence, new concepts or skills being stressed in accordance with student success in previously introduced sequence steps as well as provision made for any needed supplementary help that may exist with individual students.

This effort to identify some of the basic skills in readiness and suggest instructional techniques with their possible application through various media has been partially motivated by the writer's observations and evaluation of pupil needs in summer school remedial reading classes and through the attempt to consider individual differences and their accompanying rates of learning and also to provide interesting challenge, needed repetition and sequential skill steps in the learning activities for mentally retarded children. The majority of the retarded children fell within the "trainable" range, but some were on the borderline between the trainable and educable classifications. All had been diagnosed as having an intelligence quotient in the fifty to sixty range or below.

The mentally retarded children, their growth varying according to individual potential, length of time in the classroom, ability to concentrate and control their hyperactivity and distractibility, and other influences upon their performance, have been able to acquire many of the readiness skills. Their performance has been so encouraging and seemingly significant that there is an apparent need for more research into the individual skill areas and effort to determine how much can be accomplished by these children in certain learning areas. There is a need for more instructional research and attempts to measure and evaluate personality growth, pupil attitudes, and self-confidence possibly gained through growth in competence, skill achievement and task completion.

It seems possible that if the retarded students can make progress in some of these skills and reach a level of success in certain areas of readiness as defined by the standardized readiness tests, other students who possess more mental ability, but are delayed or deficient in needed skills may also profit from a more step-by-step skill presentation with the needed allowance of time for growth. These students need a program that provides preventive measures that will insure their meeting in the future less reading difficulties that may be resulting from their lack of readiness.

When the need is considered for any child to profit from a more meaningful curriculum which permits him to grow as he is ready and causes new learning to be in accordance with his individual needs and interests, the necessity for sequential skill development as an aspect of the retarded child's instruction cannot be neglected. Perhaps the lives of the mentally retarded children may for their present and future be more productive and happier if, through the described sequential skill development, they have learned to do the following:

1. Understand directions when given in group activities as well as to one's self individually.
2. Make one's needs and wishes known through verbal skills.
3. Use language to communicate and converse with others, to understand and be understood.
4. *Listen and look,* then perform as instructions and demonstrations are presented.
5. Maintain an interest and attention span.
6. Control one's hyperactivity as much as possible.
7. Understand and follow directions.
8. See likenesses and differences and do simple sorting and matching activities.
9. See how some things are the same.
10. Make simple classifications of things that are similar.
11. See relationships.
12. See how many things are related or used together.
13. See things that comprise wholes.
14. Control one's distractibility as much as possible.
15. Learn to keep their need to complete the task uppermost in mind and to not become inattentive through interest in what someone else is doing, a temporary distraction, or other loss of interest.
16. Stay with a task and see it to completion.
17. Realize that their efforts and contributions are very important and become motivated to do their best.
18. Respect the contributions of others.
19. Work together, cooperate and share.
20. Practice safety rules in work or recreation.
21. Use materials carefully, give them proper care and store them away when not being used.
22. Work willingly and cheerfully.

23. Have a good self-concept and respect for other people.
24. Acquire worthwhile social skills.
25. Assume responsibility for their own self-care needs to the extent of their abilities.
26. Gain a favorable self-concept.

Readiness is not merely a little corner of the reading program, but is the foundation upon which reading success is built. A greater balance between preventive and remedial measures is necessary to help solve reading problems and eliminate difficulties significant to the causes of the staggering yearly number of student school dropouts.

The plan of this book is to provide an exploration of certain readiness areas and suggest possible solutions to some problems of the students who are not ready for the necessary beginning reading skills. The needs of the different groups of students will be considered, because whatever may be the reasons, if a child lacks any of the competencies involved in reading readiness, he should have help to acquire the needed skills. Student needs will be presented, then possible instructional techniques and devices designed to accomplish specific readiness achievement will be suggested. Special application to the several groups of students will be described, but the techniques and instructional aids may also be applied in different ways to provide for other pupil needs. Although the techniques may be devoted to particular purposes in meeting the needs of children in various levels, the unique instructional aim *planned for the individual pupil* influences and helps to determine the effectiveness of the techniques and materials in accordance with pupil growth.

Some of the specific learning needs of the retarded children will be considered through suggestions for special instructional materials and techniques. The likenesses of these students to other children and also their differences enable them to profit from many of the same materials that are helpful to other children if the use of these instructional media is planned according to teacher awareness of these handicapped students' unique learning needs. Here, also, the difference lies in the need and purpose for instruction. A pre-reader in the regular classroom may need to acquire more skill in visual discrimination to help alleviate his readiness deficiency. An educable retarded child's purpose for the need to master visual skills may be also to achieve readiness according to his reading potential, but a trainable retarded child needs visual discrimination ability in preparing to accomplish simple sorting tasks, read some safety and other functional words, and to become more aware of his environment. The difference lies in pupil needs and realistic goals, as well as the special application of instructional measures.

The disadvantaged children also have a learning handicap that requires special remedial instruction before they can be exposed to any reading expectations. Some suggestions are presented for providing the necessary experiential background and its resulting conceptual vocabulary.

Classroom action research is needed to determine the effectiveness of materials and instructional techniques, and also to evaluate them as they are used with the children.

Special testing techniques are needed to determine the learning needs of the disadvantaged children and to realize the type and degree of their learning handicaps. Preventive measures through the Head Start Program are being offered to preschool children, but corrective efforts are necessary for those children who are now being confronted by reading difficulties due to their previous inadequate readiness preparation.

More awareness and preparation for the few experience-starved and vocabulary-limited children to be found in many kindergarten and first grade classrooms, even though they may not live in what is considered a culturally deprived area, must be made possible. Many classrooms contain the child who has never been to a zoo, the public library or other experience-building community centers. Many children are deprived in many other pertinent areas that influence their reading performance.

Readiness must be permitted both the needed instruction and time to develop, and the child needs this skill mastery before he is to be confronted with the additional requirements involved in formal reading. It is necessary for educators to strive to have more balance between what is realized as necessary and what is actually done to allow the child to progress at his own rate, read when he is ready, and approach reading with confidence and competence.

This author's purpose is the attempt to contribute some suggested instructional measures for providing this needed readiness through a variety of possible approaches afforded by various specific instructional techniques and learning aids.

Chapter II

SPECIAL NEEDS OF TRAINABLE CHILDREN

A COMPARISON WAS MADE at the Maplewood School in Garden City, Michigan, of a class of kindergarten students and one of retarded children ranging from intelligence scores in the fifties down into the trainable range as they responded to the same specially planned and prepared instructional materials and techniques. The comparison involved observations of their likenesses and differences in performance as compared with those of the kindergarteners.

The observers were the teacher of the kindergarten class and the special education teacher. Criteria for the evaluation related to instructional materials, pupil response, and performance of both pupil groups.

Apparently the performance of both groups of children was influenced by many of the same factors, such as mental ability, chronological age, length of time in school, attention span, kinds of instructional materials, techniques, co-ordination skills, interest, and the experiential background of the child. The performance was not always influenced in the same way for both groups of children.

Although the retarded children seemed to perform in many ways like the kindergarteners, they differed more regarding *what* skills they could learn than in *how* they responded or in the *degree* of their response. Although they differed in what skills they could perform, there was no apparent qualitative difference between the retarded children's performance in the areas in which they were successful and that of the kindergarten children in those same skills.

Trainable retarded children are most limited in their potential and in their rates of learning. They may have other physical, social and emotional handicaps, and may suffer from visual and auditory defects, cardiac disabilities, and may have speech handicaps. The clinical aspects of their types of injury may influence their ability to learn in some ways, and may be significant to how they respond.

9

In these ways, they are different in learning ability from other children because of these influences upon what they can learn: however the ways in which they learn are possibly more similar to than different from those of other children.

In planning a program for trainable children, it is necessary to consider their many present needs and limitations and how these influence their total lives. The trainable child is defined as one who is not educable to the extent that he can become self-supporting at the adult level. He will require some care, supervision, and economic support throughout his life.

> The trainable child ". . . has potentialities for learning (1) self-care, (2) social adjustment in the family and neighborhood, and (3) economic usefulness in the home, in a residential school, or in a sheltered workshop."[1]

Apparently educators should be even more concerned with the qualitative aspect of the learning of these children, as well as that of others. Results of learning are knowledge and understanding, mastery of skills, achievement, behavioral changes, attitudes, appreciation and many others. Positive manifestations of learning are made tangible through individual accomplishments, contribution to society, personal success and happiness. People are often remembered or considered outstanding for what they do, the quality of their contribution, how they influence others, and not necessarily for how much they do for the sake of quantity alone. Edward Everett's speech at Gettysburg surpassed Lincoln's in length and quantity, but the qualitative difference between the President's "few remarks" and the main speaker's oration caused the former's address to become an always existing tribute to courage and sacrifice for one's country and a comfort to the bereaved of all wars.

If trainable children showed difference merely in the quantity of their learning, educating them would be much easier. The need would be only to find the extent of their capabilities and to help them accordingly. The "how much" aspect of their differences is not as complex as the "how" they learn, and the "what." Their

---

[1]From Samuel Kirk, Winford Kirk and Merle Karnes: *You and Your Retarded Child,* 1955, p. 10. Courtesy of the Macmillan Company, New York.

qualitative differences cause difficulty in meeting all of the unique needs of each child, and are a great concern of the teacher. Their differences lie in how they acquire individual skills, how their experiences influence their attitudes, and the behaviorial changes that result from their learning. They differ in the extent to which they can communicate what they have learned, how they feel and think.

They differ also in what they can learn, length of time required for learning and response to instructional media and techniques. Their accompanying physical and emotional problems cause them to have additional needs. It is important for none of their handicaps in one area to be permitted to interfere with their opportunities to learn other skills. They may need much additional individual help. A child who may be able to perform a finer visual discrimination task, yet whose poor motor ability may hinder his performance in manipulative activities should be given special attention to prevent his coordination handicap from interfering with his learning in the other areas.

The children differ in what skills they learn. This is true of a comparison of their learning with that of other mentally handicapped children as well as with those in the regular classroom. This difference may be due to mental ability, chronological age, causes of retardation, and others. They differ in the many ways that possibly cause all children to differ plus the implications of numerous mental, physical and emotional problems that may confront them. There exists a need to know more about how their handicaps affect the quality of their individual performances and the extent of their abilities. Marion White McPherson suggests the need for openmindedness and the importance of not using only one measurement of their capabilities.

> There is evidence that the intellectual level is not an adequate predictor of the learning of mental defectives and that their learning *per se* is variable.[2]

Individual trainable retarded children can become very proficient

---

[2]From Marion White McPherson: Learning and mental deficiency. *American Journal of Mental Deficiency* March, 1958, Vol. 62, No. 5, p. 877.
Courtesy of The American Association on Mental Deficiency.

in some certain skills. A child whose birth history indicates brain injury, may be able to express himself well verbally through a very extensive vocabulary, while another though quite limited in language verbal skills, may be able to distinguish differences and likenesses in close rows of very small lower-case letters and words. Their differences cannot be merely quantitative when they can master some skills to such degrees. They differ in the what, and not merely the how much. If their differences were just quantitative, it seems that they would then be more alike in their limitations concerning all skills. Their differences are most apparent in what skills they can master, the degree of their learning, rate of learning, reinforcement and repetition necessary, and their individual responses.

The differences in their backgrounds of experiences which they can utilize to their advantage are evident in their performance. A little boy afflicted with mongolism, whose parents have permitted him to share many experiences including trips, the cottage and lake in the summer, eating in restaurants, etc., has a wealth of mental images at his command. He can form vivid sensory images and share them through "Academy Award" performances and dramatizations complete with sound effects. Still, another child who may possess less mental competence and have severe language disability may not be able to indicate what she thinks, remembers or has shared through the ways in which the other child is so expressive even though the parent provided background of experiences may be as complete. This child may differ in many other ways.

In the chart (see Table I), contrasting the quantitative and qualitative differences of two retarded children, more extensive differences exist in *areas* than in *degrees*. In the skills acquired by both, their performance was fairly similar. David, who has limited language skills, could not retell stories, yet he could otherwise indicate that he understood them.

TABLE I

Qualitative Differences	David	Gary
Self-care skills	Excellent	Fair
Attention span	Fairly consistent	Erratic
Language skills	Poor	Excellent

(continued)

TABLE 1 *(continued)*

Qualitative Differences	David	Gary
Work habits	Excellent	Fair
Ability to concentrate	Excellent	Fair
Control of distractibility	Good	Poor
Ability to follow directions	Excellent	Fair
Word matching	Excellent	Poor
Sight vocabulary	38 words	None
Rote counting	30	12
Recognition of numbers	A few	A few
Retelling a simple story	Poor	Fair
Singing	Fair	Good
Coloring	Good	Fair
Puzzles	Excellent	Good
Quantative differences in IQ. performances	50	52

Although their differences may have both qualitative and quantitative aspects there should be provision for their types of differences as well as their likenesses to other children. An awareness of the quantitative difference in their mental abilities necessitates an endeavor to plan for their later lives and to provide continued guidance and assistance. The implications of the qualitative differences in their learning characteristics signify the need to help each child to develop all of his potentialities and strive to provide instruction to meet all of his individual needs and remain continually aware of student differences.

Student #1

C.A.-11-1   M.A.-2-9   I.Q.-33
Test—Stanford-Binet, Form L
Birthday—5/7/52   Years in Trainable Class—2½
Etiological and other factors—Mongolism and articulatory defects

Self-care Skills

1. Can dress himself, manage boots and other apparel.
2. Manages well in eating; uses silverware at home, assumes care of own lunch preparation, such as opening milk, thermos, etc. at school.
3. Plays safely in room and on playground.
4. Uses handkerchief.
5. Goes to lavatory alone and comes back to the room promptly.

Social Adjustment
1. Uses words of courtesy, and is considerate of others.
He comforts other children who may be hurt or crying.
He shares toys, etc.
2. Can participate in class programs.
3. Assumes responsibilities in emergency drills; closes windows and doors for fire drills.
4. Can do errands that require going to other parts of the building.

Economic Usefulness
1. Hangs up own clothes, keeps room neat, etc.
2. Sets the table at home.
3. Helps with school lunch time preparation; passes straws, milk, etc.
4. Uses broom well and can dust.
5. Brings notes to school and home and can bring his money.

Readiness Growth
1. Has completed many of the activities in several readiness workbooks. Has a sight vocabulary of twenty-six words (safety and color words, children's names, etc.).
2. Can rote count to ten and recognize some of the number symbols.
3. Can trace, color and do art activities. Can use scissors.
4. Can print his first name.
5. Can do musical games, dances, exercises, etc. by self and with others.
6. Can do physical education activities; bat a ball, walk the coordination railroad track, "shoot" a ball into the basketball net, run races, etc.

Readiness Test Record
Lee-Clark Readiness Test
Letter Symbols—Matching and Cross Out   Rating: High
Vocabulary and Following Directions
Identification of Letters and Words
Total Rating: High Avg.
Grade Placement Equivalent: 0.8
Expectation of Success: Excellent
Delay Indicated: None
Ginn Pre-reading Test
Vocabulary Readiness: Scored 13 from possible 16
Visual Readiness: Scored 8 from possible 15

Tactile-Visual Readiness: Scored 14 from possible 15
Comprehension Readiness: Scored 4 from possible 8

Student #2

C.A.   10-1   M.A.   4-6   I.Q.-50
Test—Stanford-Binet, Form L
Goodenough
Birthday—6/13/53   Years in Trainable Class—2
Other Factors—Speech difficult to understand
                          Short attention span
                          Hyperactivity

Self-care Skills
1. Assumes responsibility for dressing himself at home, can manage boots, etc. Can tie shoes. Hangs up coat, etc. Helps to keep room neat.

Social Adjustment
1. Works, plays, shares well with others.
2. Very dependable. Helps to keep the classroom floor neat by putting toys away after play, picking up scraps after art activities, etc. Loves to assume responsibility.
3. Can finish what he starts and stick to a task well.

Reading Readiness
1. Can match words that are alike and different.
2. Can recognize by sight the words in the preprimers, *We Look and See and We Work and Play.*
3. Can do activities in the readiness workbooks.
4. Listens to and enjoys stories.

Arithmetic Readiness
1. Can count to thirty with some help.
2. Can recognize number symbols to ten.
3. Uses some numbers in daily experiences.
4. Can write number symbols to ten.

Penmanship Readiness
1. Can trace, color and use scissors.
2. Cuts and pastes.
3. Does well in handicraft activities.
4. Can print his first name.

Physical Education
1. Can follow rules for group games.
2. Can march, skip, dance, etc.
3. Can play basketball, walk balance board, etc.

Loves to sing, paint, and do art projects.

Readiness Test Record

    Lee-Clark Reading Readiness Test

    Letter Symbols—Matching and Cross Out   Rating: High Avg.

    Vocabulary and Following Directions   Rating: Low Avg.

    Word Symbols   Rating: High

    Total Rating: High Avg.

    Grade Placement Equivalent: 1.0

    Expectation of Success: Good

    Delay Indicated: None

    Ginn Pre-reading Test

    Vocabulary Readiness: Perfect Score

    Visual Readiness: Scored 12 from possible 15

    Tactile-Visual Readiness: Scored 11 from possible 15

    Comprehension Readiness: Scored 5 from possible 8

Chapter III

THE EDUCABLE RETARDED CHILD

The educable retarded child is one who, because of slow mental development, is unable to profit sufficiently from the program of the regular elementary school. He is able to learn some of the academic skills such as reading, writing and arithmetic. This is why he is called "educable." He can probably acquire second, third, or fourth grade achievement at the age of sixteen. He can learn to work and in most cases can become self-supporting at the adult level.[3]

These boys and girls are not mentally incompetent. Comparing their minds to an engine we would say they have a slower dynamo than the average child, but it is a good dynamo. They do, however, need specialized methods and techniques and a program suited to their needs. This program should be a realistic, meaningful presentation of the academic work which will equip them to handle their daily tasks.[4]

ALTHOUGH THE EDUCABLE retarded child will require special application of a readiness program to meet his educational, personal, social and emotional needs, it is first necessary to gain a valid assessment of his mental abilities through an adequate psychological evaluation. This testing should reveal his age, intelligence quotient, and a measurement of verbal and perceptual skills and other thought processes. In school systems where there are the available services of a psychologist, referrals may be made by the classroom teacher if additional special help seems needed by a child. The aid of child guidance clinics may be sought through the visiting teacher or school social worker or by the classroom teacher if this help is needed to evaluate pupil needs.

Visual and Hearing Tests

Visual and hearing tests may be provided through the aid of the

---

[3]Samuel Kirk, Winford Kirk, and Merle Karnes, *loc. cit.,* p. 9.
[4]From Marian Smith: *Teaching the Slow Learning Child,* 1954, p. 8. Courtesy of Harper and Row Publishers, Inc. New York.

city or county health department. This testing is imperative if the areas of the child's handicap are to be identified and provided for. Many school systems arrange for vision and hearing testing to be administered by a vision screening technician and an ophthalmologist or hearing clinic for diagnosis and recommend treatment.

Cumulative Records

Pertinent information to be included in the child's *cumulative school record consists* of an adequate up-to-date appraisal of the child's health, family, siblings, and a thorough progress report concerning his school performance. These are the general areas of needed information, but there are other kinds of information that can have special implications for enabling the teacher to better understand and help the child. Some of these are as follows below.

Anecdotal Records

1. *The anecdotal record* by the teacher should contain anything done or said by the child that seems to indicate how he feels about himself, his school or home life, and not only his attitude about others but also how he thinks others feel about him. The apparently belligerent child who says he hates reading in the remedial class often gains benefit from special help to permit him to gain more competence. Praise and encouragement will help him to gain self-respect and confidence in his ability. This personal growth will then contribute to his reading improvement.

Other Information

Sometimes the chance statement can give the teacher a helpful lead concerning circumstances that may be contributing to his school problem. A boy in a summer school remedial reading class asked the teacher if he could leave his new book on her desk after each class session because his little brothers and sisters would destroy it. Through a discussion with him, the teacher found that he was in the middle age-range of a family of twelve children. Since several siblings were older than he, this boy had never enjoyed the status position of being one of the older family members. He felt no confidence in his ability to be considered responsible or "grown up." Several younger children were "always messing up my things, sleeping in the same room with me, making noise, getting in my hair," and so on according to the boy's complaint. This gave the teacher much insight and understanding of possible reasons why the boy had difficulty concentrating in class written work, listening, and seeing assignments through to completion. This information was shared with the other teacher in whose class the boy was also having difficulty with written assignments as well as being below grade level in basic skills.

Progress Reports

2. *The teacher-witten progress reports* needed in addition to the child's report-card appraisal of performance should contain not only the areas of difficulty with study skills, behavioral problems and apparent performance below grade level, but also reasons or even "hunches" that suggest possible reasons for these problems. How the child seems to feel about the situation should also be included as well as the teacher's observations. What has been tried to meet the need even if these attempts resulted in failure should be recorded. Any suggestions that are considered possible solutions or ways of dealing with the child's problem would also be very valuable to the next teacher and should be included. Observations and findings concerning parental attitudes or information that has been gathered through parent conferences are important.

Parent-teacher Conferences

3. *Summaries* of what has taken place during *parent-teacher conferences* should be included. Follow-up reports should list results of teacher and parent plans made during conferences. Evaluations of what was or was not done and how this affected the problem would be helpful.

Parent Guidance

4. Records of guidance and help that has been given to parents would contribute to the effort to continue needed parental guidance.

Other Agencies

5. If suggestions have been sent to the school from *outside*

agencies whose help has been sought, there should be a record of how these suggestions were followed and their contribution to the effort to meet the child's need.

The utilization of this information will be helpful to the teacher also as the referral to seek additional special help is prepared.

A prolonged and enriched readiness program is needed especially by the educable retarded child to enable him to not be exposed to reading until he is ready.

> A retarded child whose age may be six, seven, eight or even nine should not be introduced to a systematic reading program. He should be given a reading readiness program.[5]

A readiness program that insures the child's success through the sequential skill presentation and repetition afforded by interesting supplementary activities to reinforce previously taught skills when necessary is especially important for the retarded child whose self-confidence, effort and consequently his performance are in jeopardy if he fails in reading as a result of inadequate preparation. The program of instruction must be at his level if he is to read with success and feel pride in his ability.

> Encouragement is more effective with retarded children than it is with superior children. These children should be encouraged by the teacher and the knowledge of their own success.[6]

Other child-development goals in addition to the academic skills that are possible for the educable retarded child through the readiness program are the following.

Mental Health

1. Helping the child to feel secure and adequate through his achieving at his level and making a worthwhile contribution to group living.

2. Helping him share in easy but challenging activities; thus, encouraging him to continually strive to improve and keep trying.

---

[5]From Samuel and Orville Johnson: *Educating the Retarded Child,* 1951, p. 256. Courtesy of The Houghton Mifflin Company, 2 Park Street, Boston 7.

Attitudes and Habits

1. Helping him to share, cooperate and respect others as he works and plays with them.

2. Learning to wait until others have a turn, being kind and considerate to others.

Language Development

1. Increasing his verbal ability to use words to express what he wishes to communicate.

2. Using words and their meanings to describe, classify, compare, tell picture stories, indicate pictures to show meanings, etc.

Social Participation and Adjustment:

1. To help the child to gain responsibility and independence to the extent of his capabilities by being responsible for his part in activities and learning to be responsible for equipment and materials during and after use.

2. Learning to utilize materials that are available in one's home such as plastic cartons, buttons and other scrap items to be used in preparing readiness devices.

3. Learning to share responsibility and materials with others.

4. Learning to participate with others in group projects, yet be responsible for one's independent work and assignments, too.

5. Learning to follow directions and assume one's responsibilities in a work or activity situation.

6. Learning to work with a group of others, to be a cheerful worker, and to be dependable.

7. Learning to be punctual and to complete tasks or activities on time.

8. Learning to stay on the job and to accept one's responsibilities concerning how well it is done, pride in achievement.

9. Learning to accept and utilize suggestions and criticisms.

10. Learning to control one's temper and have patience.

Parent Education Programs

There is even more need for parent education programs concerning the educable retarded child than there is for parents of

---

[6]Kirk, Samuel, and Irene Stevens: A pre-academic curriculum for slow-learning children. *The American Journal of Mental Deficiency, April,* 1943, Vol. 47, No. 4.

children in the regular grades. Too often, the parents of educable children who are attending segregated classes do not participate in the parent-teacher association activities in the building where their child's class is housed and they do not realize the need for their own special parent education as those parents of trainable children often do. Their child is not handicapped to the extent that the trainable child is, and since he is educable, there may be a danger of too high parental hopes and plans for his future. The pupil learning/handicap must be interpreted so that parents will be able to understand and accept the fact that they cannot plan for this child to choose a profession that involves a college education, but that he needs guidance and vocational training as well as help in preparing for a job placement.

The educable adult will need much less external support than the trainable person. The educable retarded learner can potentially support himself, but will need some follow-up guidance and help even after job placement following a job training and orientation experience. Parents of trainable children need to realize how much effort is being put forth to treat and prevent retardation and also to seek educational methods for helping their child to assume responsibilities in accordance with his abilities. There is a need for parents to plan for their child's future, too, and realize that the situation for the present indicates the probable need for his external support and guidance throughout his adult life. Continued counseling and interpreting their child's needs are necessary to help the parent in accomplishing this planning and the necessary action.

Parents wish to know that everything possible is being done to help their child. When they realize how the school and home are a team to work together for their child's benefit, needed planning and action are easier to undertake, whether this consists of helping the little one learn to put on his own boots, encouraging and expecting him to help with chores in the home or placing his name on a waiting list for future residential care in preparation for a possible time to come when he cannot be cared for by the family.

Many parents receive needed emotional support and form new friendships with others through the parent education program where their talking about and sharing mutual fears and feelings or offering suggestions ("Well, I had that problem with Sally, too, but when I tried this, it helped.") to each other over the coffee cup often contribute as much to their benefit as the words of the evening speaker.

Chapter IV

THE CHILD WHO IS DELAYED IN READINESS SKILLS

T HERE IS FOUND in many first-grade classrooms a small but significant number of beginners who have not reached the level of growth needed to achieve successfully in reading. They may fall into the categories of "Delayed One Year or More" or "Poor Risk" according to the results of the readiness tests that are administered at the beginning of the first grade year.

As reading is presented to the class, these children often lag exceedingly far behind their more competent classmates, and after various regroupings as the class moves forward in the reading program, the delayed beginners may not really "fit" into any of the reading groups. The discrepancy between what is expected of them and what they can do begins to continually widen as the skills become more abundant and progressively difficult. These children begin to become more aware of their failure and their lack of self-confidence may prevent their showing effort even when what is expected may be within their levels of ability.

The lack of growth by these delayed beginners was perhaps apparent even during their kindergarten year. They were probably not successful in the readiness activities at the latter part of that year, and were perhaps found "not ready for readiness," as a teacher described this small group in her class of kindergarteners. Although a variety of activities may have been shared by the class, these same few were found at the bottom of the class success totem pole too often.

Failure of these children may be evident and observed by their teacher as pupil progress is evaluated in several areas.

1. *Leadership Ability:* Failure may be apparent in their lack of leadership or initiative as they attempt to participate in group games that require following directions, sharing turns and remem-

24

bering rules and words to be chanted or sung. They may be unable to set goals for their own accomplishment or to use their free time effectively.

2. *Individual Needs:* Some of these children may usually and repetitively choose the same activity during free-choice periods to fill one deprived need. A teacher of a kindergarten class observed that one little girl always chose to cut out pictures from magazines or construction paper during the activity period and at any other time possible during the day. This child's need was understood by her teacher who was aware of the fact that there was little opportunity for her to cut out pictures or otherwise use scissors at home, and there had apparently been no encouragement or permission for this need to be provided for during the little girl's preschool years.

3. *Behavioral Reactions:* The delayed beginners may be restless and hyperactive or unable to exercise self-control sufficiently to assume responsibility for working purposefully toward accomplishing a goal or completing a task. They may need much more supportive help from the teacher than the other children do. Their attention and interest span may be very short, and frequent changes of activities may be needed to renew their lagging interest. These children may need much positive direction from the teacher to help them learn to concentrate and listen during class activities. Such directions as, "Put your hands in your lap and get ready to listen as Billy names these zoo animals," or, "It's Jim's turn now, but in a few minutes I'll call on you, Joe, so be ready," may have to be given often to these beginners who need definite help in developing habits of self-control.

4. *Work Habits:* Some children may be unable to assume responsibility for working independently, or they may work so slowly and painstakingly that when their classmates are finished with one activity and are ready to do something else, the slower students may have only started. Their extremely short span of interest and concentration may prevent their staying with a task for a sufficient length of time, and they often give up in discouragement.

5. *Play Characteristics:* Their play may be only at the solitary or parallel levels because group games may require concentration, sharing and waiting for turns, social maturity characterized by a

secure sense of belonging to the group, and leadership abilities not possessed by many of these slower learners. Supportive help and leadership from an adult can promote their learning to play if they are encouraged to wait for a turn and be responsible for their share in the game. Sufficient time and encouragement must be permitted. The child who enjoys success in group play will in turn want to play more often in this manner, and will then become more competent.

6. *Creative Play and Dramatization:* The delayed beginners may enjoy expression of their individual imaginative ability to "make up" their own games or entertainment; however, they may lack sufficient leadership ability and influence to involve their classmates to a very great extent in this play. The teacher may help by giving much encouragement and many opportunities for creative play, dramatization and other possibilities for each child's talents to be revealed and appreciated. Opportunities for simple dramatic play may be encouraged by, (a) dramatizing pictures that suggest a story. Pictures that relate to everyday experiences that are understood by the children should be used. Examples are a little girl dressing up in her mother's clothes or a boy helping his little brother learn to cross a street. Simple costume or property needs for this dramatization can easily be obtained, yet they mean so much. A shy child can become a new and more confident person by "being" someone else in the "play," and (b) the availability of various toys that motivate dramatic expression, such as telephones, puppets, trucks, fire engines, dolls, and dishes, helps to stimulate spontaneous dramatic play ideas. Clothing may be kept available for "dress up" play.

7. *Verbal Expression:* The background of experiences shared by the delayed beginner may be very meager. This child may not be able to express himself well verbally to answer questions, describe an experience or retell a story. Such activities as these should be based upon the child's individual interests and background. Awareness of individual needs and differences will permit the teacher to accomplish this more to the child's advantage.

8. *Coordination Skills:* Many of the delayed beginners may have poor motor and eye-hand coordination. This may be reflected in their coloring and drawings and lack of penmanship readiness.

Games requiring motor and eye-hand coordination skills are difficult for these children to participate in successfully. They profit from individual help to develop the eye-hand coordination and finer muscular skills needed to perform these tasks.

9. *Emotional Needs:* Many children who lack readiness competencies need additional emotional support from the teacher to help them to overcome their fears and feelings of inadequacy. They must have encouragement and warm acceptance of their contributions with persistent praise and motivation to put forth their best efforts. This acceptance must be balanced by clearly defined limits, directions and structured activities containing goals that are satisfying to the children. Kindly firmness and insistence upon their adherence to the rules and routines that are defined in accordance with their needs may be accompanied by warm enthusiasm and praise for their efforts and achievements. High expectations that require the pupils' highest achievement should also be followed by praise, and recognition or emotional support when this is needed.

It often appears that no matter what is done by the class group, the delayed beginners are unable to make a good showing in the opinions of their peers, and also as important, in their own concepts of themselves. Although it may often be true that "nothing succeeds like success," for the delayed child who is not ready for readiness activities, the story is often reversed to, "nothing fails like failure."

The above described characteristics do not all apply to any one child. A student may be very handicapped in some skill areas and successful in others, while other children may not seem to be able to really do anything well.

The range of individual differences in this group of children is as broad as it is to be found within any classroom. All students do not lack social competence, but some may. Some may be very popular with their classmates while others are shy and timid. If it could be said of any group, "They are like that," perhaps teaching would be much easier and less challenging. In many instances, when considering student likenesses to other children, the teacher can think of the "they" in attempting to determine pupil needs and evaluate pupil growth. When considering their differences, however, there may be a thoughtful, "He can't seem to master this skill now," "She needs more readiness help in this way," "The possible solution for Bill's problem may be accomplished if I try this," etc.

A Pupil Problem

Ronnie's apparent slowness was noticed first by his kindergarten teacher, and her reference to this was included in his record folder. The teacher of first grade observed that he could not tell or otherwise indicate likenesses and differences in pictures or comprehend the story sequence depicted by a series of pictures. Ronnie could not visualize the parts missing from pictured objects. His verbal vocabulary was very limited, and he rarely spoke in complete sentences. The delay indicated by his reading readiness test result was one year or more, and his expected success in reading was very poor. Although the mental maturity test that was administered to the group by the teacher placed his intelligence quotient at ninety-two, the child's marked lack of reading readiness in so many areas seemed indicative of the need for special help.

Socially, Ronnie was accepted very well by his class. The other children were eager for him to succeed and were lavish with their praise and encouragement. His being in the class with the same classmates over the two-year period had resulted in a strong protective attitude toward him by the other children, and this was manifested in continued awareness of his needs and willingness to help him. During his first-grade year, he stayed with the regular class, but was given the opportunity to proceed at his own level through much individual help and adjustment of his curriculum goals in accordance with his abilities. Later, as the discrepancy between his chronological and mental age widened and reading skills became more compelling, he was placed in the type A segregated classroom program for mildly mentally retarded children.

Individual Pupil Differences

Some of the slower learners may be very imaginative and skillful in some areas. Christine, who had not mastered many of the readiness skills and was delayed according to the test evaluation, had a vivid imagination which she revealed in storytelling, puppet shows, and the class play. Dennis excelled in artistic ability, and he displayed this talent in individual projects as well as the class group mural paintings. Billy was not ready for the introduction of the preprimer skills, but his small shoulders straightened with pride and he seemed to grow taller before the eyes of his teacher who asked him to wheel the cart that transported the filmstrip projector down to the special projection room and prepare to operate it during its use with the class.

These children with special readiness needs may have some talents which enable them to "shine," while others may apparently not be able to do anything well. Whatever their abilities or weaknesses may be, if they have not achieved success in any or all of the readiness skills, they need the help and sufficient time necessary to gain the needed readiness background. Meeting their needs requires considering their strengths as well as their differences.

10. *Physical Disabilities:* There may be physical disabilities involved in the learning handicaps that hinder the children's readiness growth. Most common are auditory, visual, and speech handicaps. Through screening procedures, these needs may be discovered and provided for, the necessary referrals being made if special help is needed.

There exists the danger of the child who is delayed in readiness skills being described as "immature" before there is a thorough awareness of the implications involved in this description. The word "immature" can be a vague catch-all to include anything from unacceptable behavior, or inability to assume responsibility to non-performance or work below grade level. An unfavorable result of this word's application to the characteristics of the delayed beginner is its possible implication of a comparison of a child with his peers and not an evaluation according to his own potential. Its meaning involves too many general factors and can result in a too hasty evaluation of a student based upon insufficient information.

The causes for and the areas of the child's lack of acquisition of skills must be determined and corrected. The realization of the need for instruction to be paced according to the child's ability to receive each skill must be accompanied by actual application of this theory through instructional media and techniques. Sufficient time to meet the child's individual needs is necessary. Understanding of pupil weaknesses in skill areas will enable the teacher to prepare or obtain supplementary techniques and instructional aids to help the child in acquiring each skill before the next is introduced.

The students who are delayed in readiness lack certain necessary basic skills and abilities. They have definite skill gaps which can be filled, but this must be done through aimed instruction, and not merely "another year to mature." Until this lack is provided for, no amount of time alone to "catch-up" will be sufficient. If time and repeating grades alone could provide the solution, there would be far less students in the later elementary and high school grades reading years below their grade levels. There would not exist the present enormous school dropout problem. Basic needs necessary for readiness exist in every learning area and are influenced by individual differences in abilities, experiences in the home and school, and every aspect of the child's life. Teachers and parents can assume an important role in changing the pattern of a child's life from possible failure to success and self-esteem.

If children are to be retained at the end of kindergarten or first grade, it should be a purposeful retention based upon careful evaluation of pupil needs and definite suggestions and recommendations provided for follow-up help and special attention to needs. These retained children come labeled, "Handle with Care" because it is evident that they lack basic readiness competencies. A general retention without special emphasis upon provision for their learning handicaps, whether they exist in social skill areas, emotional needs, visual and perceptual, auditory or other readiness skills, cannot fulfill all that is required for the child to prepare for a successful and enjoyable reading experience.

Although basic needs exist in all learning areas, much of the content of this book will attempt to show how they concern reading readiness. Some of the needed prereadiness experiences for the child who, through general observation and evaluation by the teacher as well as according to the standardized tests, is found to be delayed in skills, will be presented.

It is important for teachers and parents to be more aware of the factors in pupil readiness for reading. Special consideration will be given to some of the major readiness factors in the chapters that concern instructional techniques and their application to the development of skills.

Chapter V

SPECIAL NEEDS OF CHILDREN

S PECIAL NEEDS of the learner are stressed by reading authorities and emphasized as an important factor in reading readiness. These needs include all factors involved in making reading meaningful, what reading can do to help the child achieve success in gaining knowledge, skills for use in other learning areas, and as a key to the door to the wonderful special world that only the child who reads successfully can enter.

Mental Hygiene in the Classroom

There is no greater learner need than that of mental hygiene in the classroom. Teachers have an obligation to build rapport with all children to the extent that all pupils can realize that they are important as persons whatever their abilities may be. The statement has been made that school should be a place where every child feels good about *who he is, where he is,* and *what he is.* Children with problems are often misunderstood because of behavior that they are unable to control.

Teachers often cannot change the conditions that cause pupil problems, but they can continually seek to know the individual students and to understand their problems. All problems that involve a child are the responsibility of all adults who have in any way assumed responsibility for his well-being.

Much can be accomplished through the understanding that this challenge exists and where it starts.

There are certain children in each classroom whose emotional needs cannot be met in the usual way. Studies show that about ten percent of the children in each school fall in this category. For example, in a class of thirty, there will be approximately three children who show behavior deviant enough to cause real concern to the teacher.[7]

This is not to infer that all emotionally disturbed children will become delinquent. It is to stress the fact that teachers who have the child under their care at school during his formative years have many opportunities to notice disturbed behavior, and through better understanding help to solve the child's problems and to possibly prevent some future tragedies.

The emotionally disturbed child cannot, without special help, adjust to a regular classroom. He may be working below his capacity.

> The child who is emotionally disturbed cannot concentrate. He cannot concentrate on learning because the major portion of his attention and energy is focused on how to relieve the tension caused by the emotional disturbance.[8]

Children with special emotional problems present a challenge to the teacher in the regular classroom. They may require much special attention and individual help both in the skill and learning areas and study skills. An understanding of their real needs will aid the teacher in helping them as well as maintaining classroom discipline.

> The children who have difficulties have become overwhelmed by too many obstacles. To get for themselves what a human needs, they are doing all they know how. They are fighting for their survival, and that is the cause of their misbehavior.
> 1. They may boast or bully or talk back to get a sense of their own power now because they didn't have a chance to feel big and strong when they were little.
> 2. They may interrupt or want to be right all the time, to feel important and that they can do things.[9]
> In any situation, boys and girls are striving to feel right about themselves, to feel that they have worth, to feel that they are accepted.[10]

[7]Katherine D'Evelyn: *Meeting Children's Emotional Needs: A Guide for Teachers,* 1957. Reprinted by permission of Prentice-Hall, Inc., Englewood Cliffs, New Jersey.

[8]Kimball Wiles: *Teaching for Better Schools,* 1952, p. 49. Reprinted by permisssion of Prentice-Hall, Inc., Englewood Cliffs, New Jersey.

[9]James L. Hymes Jr.: *Behavior and Misbehavior,* 1955, pp. 90-91. Reprinted by permission of Prentice-Hall, Inc., Englewood Cliffs, New Jersey.

[10]Kimball Wiles, *loc. cit.,* p. 50.

Many evidences of a possible emotional disturbance or learning problem confronting a child are often early existent. Their observance by a parent or teacher facilitates a referral for a clinical evaluation, and the recommended child guidance may then be provided. Problems that threaten the emotional health of the pupil do not suddenly loom up to threaten the child merely because he is being exposed to academic activities. Many problems begin long before the school entry. The child with special emotional needs can be noticed when he is in kindergarten, and the attempt to meet learner needs involves his type of problems, too. The mental hygiene atmosphere in the classroom contributes much toward prevention of many difficulties before they arise as well as helping to solve the child problems that are brought to school.

The teacher's general attitude toward the whole class contributes much to the success and emotional well being of all pupils. Much can be done to provide for learner needs through the following efforts:

1. Respect for each child's ability and the realization of his strengths and weaknesses.

2. Praise and encouragement of each child's efforts to contribute and share his ideas with the group.

3. Absence of force upon a child to express himself or take an active part, but the motivation and encouragement of this pupil participation.

4. Praise and examples displayed of neat work or best efforts of children are needed, and never having the attention of the class directed toward an individual's poor or incorrect work as an example. If a child seems to not be doing his best, the teacher may gain insight into causes of this inadequate performance through individual help or a private conference with the student. The pupil disinterest may be the result of a personal problem with which help is needed.

5. Planning story dramatizations for reading groups and having children participate in committees to provide needed materials and prepare for the class activities. A too shy child may begin by taking part in the committee work that does not involve speaking before the class, but later be able to volunteer for leadership roles. Working in small groups at first can help the shy child to overcome fear of taking part in larger group work.

6. If the teacher is enthusiastic and enjoys working with the class, this will provide a social norm of industry and interest.

7. When the teacher is always aware of the necessity for each child to have his own success in some way, many emotional and behavioral problems can be prevented before they become too serious.

8. Encouragement of the parents to come and visit the classroom and to help with as many activities as possible is helpful in interpreting school goals as well as for fostering pupil pride and self-concept. Parents want to help their children and need to know what ways in which they can. The child's school life must be shared with the parents, then when serious problems arise, they can more easily be solved through school and parent team effort.

Burton presented the following list as some normal emotional and social adjustments necessary to readiness:

1. Adequate emotional stability, self-control.
2. Initiative, ambition, desire to achieve.
3. Self-reliance, willingness to assume responsibility.
4. Enjoyment in associating with others, in participating in group activities.
5. Co-operative attitude, ready to respect the rights of others, to take turns, to share.
6. Courteous attitude and manners.

Favorable attitudes and interests emphasized by Burton are as follows:

1. Attitude that reading is fun, that it is useful, that it is a good thing to learn.
2. Attitude of desiring to learn to read.
3. Attitude of confidence in ability to learn to read.
4. Interest in books, especially picture-story books; desire to handle books and turn pages.
5. Interest in the identity and meaning of printed words in books, also wherever found in other places, as on the bulletin board and on signs.
6. Interest in pictures in books, also whenever found elsewhere, as in magazines and on the bulletin board.
7. Eagerness to hear stories, sufficient to ask others to tell stories or to read them aloud.

8. Desire to tell some of the best stories to others.[11]

The emotional needs of the child whose problem hinders his adjustment in the classroom so much that he cannot perform according to his potential often require a referral by the teacher for additional services available through the visiting teacher or school social worker, psychologist and health nurse. This team approach provides much more insight into the child's problem, and the observations of each of these school personnel are very valuable for use in consideration of possible solutions.

The child's self-concept is an important aspect of his personality development, and is significant to his achievement. Many children who are hindered by reading difficulties feel that they are failures. This attitude of defeat prevents their efforts to try, which in turn adversely affects their growth in ability. This continued lack of progress adds to their concept of themselves as inadequate. Reading difficulties can only be alleviated through much individual help and remedial measures. Early effort to give help at home during the preschool years and through kindergarten and first grade school experiences that promote a worthwhile pupil self-concept can help to minimize such difficulties.

Physical Needs

The learner's physical needs are necessary to reading readiness.

Some of these basic physical needs are listed below.

1. General Physical Health That Is Conducive To Learning Ability. The record of the child's physical examination by a physician with any accompanying special recommendations to the school is a basic prerequisite to the preschooler's entrance in school. Although this information is obtained by many schools previous to any child's school registration, and is considered to be a basic requirement, the progress of many children in schools located in deprived areas is hindered through inadequate record keeping, lack of health records, and laxness in forwarding school records of children who move frequently from school to school. This has been especially so for the children whose parents are migrant farm workers and move several times during a school

---

[11]From, *Reading in Child Development,* by William H. Burton. Copyright 1956 by The Bobbs-Merrill Company, Inc., reprinted by permission of the publishers.

year. Their attendance in some schools has consisted of one or two months at the most, then they were forced to move on to seek the next crop's offering of a short period of work for their parents. Cumulative records of these children's progress in school were too seldom requested at the time of their transfer.

The marked discrepancy between school standards or grade level expectations between schools in more advantaged localities and those disadvantaged areas must be provided for through special emphasis upon individual pupil needs and application of instructional techniques and curriculum goals accordingly. This need is evident when students transfer from schools in one state to another. Effort to correct these interfering factors is being shown through the activities of the Head Start programs.

2. Visual Acuity Abilities. Most schools secure the services of the local health departments in obtaining a vision screening for kindergarten children, and this program is carried on throughout the later elementary and secondary school years.

3. Auditory Abilities. Arrangements for the children to have a hearing evaluation by an audiologist may be made by the board of education through the cooperation of the health department.

These physical readiness needs are included in the Ginn Pre-Reading Rating Scale suggested for teacher use. Questions to be considered by the teacher in rating the child in each of the areas of pre-reading skills are included in this questionnaire. Other areas included in the Ginn Rating Scale are as follows:

  a. Facility in Oral Language
  b. Concept and Vocabulary Development
  c. Listening Abilities
  e. Visual Discrimination
  f. Auditory Perception
  g. Social Skills
  h. Emotional Development
  i. Attitude toward and Interest in Reading
  j. Work Habits
  k. Muscular Coordination,[12]

---

[12]Clymer, Theodore, Christenson, Bernice M., and Russell, David H.: *Manual for Building Pre-reading Skills, Kit A Language.* 1965, pp. 8. Published by Ginn and Company Boston, Mass. Used with permission.

General areas that require instruction to develop specific readiness skills, such as visual discrimination and language skills, will be considered in detail later in the chapters relating to instructional techniques.

4. There are *aesthetic needs* of the child to be provided for through opportunities to appreciate beauty. The school must give special consideration to what is lacking in the lives of the children whose homes do not contain books, magazines, or other evidences of an environment that can contribute to readiness for reading. Many children in disadvantaged areas have few experiences such as listening to fine music or appreciation of great art masterpieces. Too often, these children must hear sounds to indicate that which is frightening or harmful, or those noises that are only more evidences of their drab surroundings.

5. Other special needs of children include a *background of experiences* upon which concepts may be built. This must be provided by both the home and school, and through a variety of experiences and activities. Concept development and vocabulary building are one of the basic principles of the pre-reading program suggested in the Ginn pre-reading manual.

> Concepts, which are ideas representing a class of things, events, or characteristics, may be considered the building blocks of reading comprehension. Since words may be thought of as the labels applied to concepts, vocabulary merits careful attention in pre-reading instruction. Although some children may bring to school well-developed concepts and an extensive speaking and listening vocabulary, other children will need special guidance and instruction to strengthen their impoverished conceptual development and to enrich their vocabularies.[13]

6. *Skill in speech* to enable the child to easily communicate and be understood by others is necessary to reading readiness.

This speech skill also includes fluency to permit the child to describe or retell in his own words what he has heard or experienced.

The school speech therapist may serve as consultant in making

---

[13]Clymer, Christenson, and Russsell: *Manual for Building Pre-reading Skills, Kit A. Ibid.*, p. 2.

recommendations to the classroom teacher regarding possibilities for supplementary help that may be provided for the children who are receiving help through the speech program. This help may concern needs in vocabulary building and auditory discrimination and other areas as well as problems relating to speech production.

The needs described herein have concerned all children generally. Those relating to specific readiness skills will be presented more fully in the chapter sections involving the trainable and educable mentally retarded, the disadvantaged and other pre-reading students.

Chapter VI

READINESS SKILL AREAS

M ORE UNDERSTANDING of the relationship and significance of the readiness skills to reading abilities is needed. A comprehensive presentation of all that is involved in reading readiness with emphasis upon the need for step-by-step pacing of these skills for the children who require this slower paced instruction has contribution to offer to the prevention of some pupil failures in reading. The resulting loss of pupil self-confidence, the disinterest in reading, and apathetic or open refusal to read may be prevented.

Knowledge of the basic skills and developmental sequence in reading readiness is necessary for all who are preparing to teach whether it is to be in the elementary schools or high school subject areas. The developmental skill aspect of readiness applies to all grade level or subject areas. Realization of this is necessary for diagnosis of pupil needs and providing adequate instructional measures whether this be in planning for high school English or history students or pre-readers. Teacher ability to look at *children* rather than grade levels is necessary for applying remedial help wherever needed; high school or elementary classes. The prereading school activities of the child are so vital to his successful preparation that in addition to the general planning of instructional aims in lesson plans, the teacher of kindergarten or first grade may do well to ask, "For what reading skill is this lesson preparing this child?" Thus, help can be provided through prevention of some reading difficulties.

This writing will not claim to contain all of the readiness skills, but only some of the important areas will be presented in this chapter and others in the sections describing the materials used with kindergartners, suggestions for parents, and the contributions of audiovisual aids to developing competence in readiness skills. Some skills that are merely mentioned in this section will be emphasized in sequential steps later when the use of instructional techniques is described. In some cases, the reading abilities that are dependent upon pupil mastery of readiness skills will be included.

Language Skills

1. Ability To Recognize Pictured Objects

Actual expriences are the most effective means for increasing the child's conceptual vocabulary, but much can be done to supplement them through the use of pictures, magazines, first dictionaries, and also picture and story books. The beginner should be helped in learning the verbal symbol that applies to each picture. He may, as directed, point to pictures and indicate those named by the teacher or parent. Many children who are delayed in reading skills are limited in vocabulary. A boy in a second grade reading class was receiving help from a tutor to correct some of his reading difficulties. When asked to name the pictures in the workbook, he called a fireplace a "firehouse" a cow was called a "sheep," and he could not distinguish between a hoe and a rake.

Special attention is needed by many children in mastery of words that are similar in meaning *(large* and *big,* and *small,* etc.). Various meanings that apply to the same word need to be presented and explained, such as two meanings for "left." This instruction should be continuous as the meanings become more complex and numerous. Children who are limited in their storehouse of word meanings will have trouble using context clues and comprehension skills for use in recognizing and understanding words when they are used in a setting different from the familiar one.

The child's vocabulary of words that describe size, actions and sounds needs to be increased. Many opportunities for verbal comparisons and contrasts may be provided through teacher and pupil discussions relating to meaningful activities and experiences. A child who cannot recall the verbal symbols for naming the pictures in his workbook will have added difficulties when attempting to identify the initial sounds for these pictured objects for use in word-attack.

2. Ability To Use Sentences

Shane and his co-authors emphasized receptive skills of listening related to reading ability and the expressive skills involved in speaking and writing as well as how these skills begin at the readiness level.

> Even at the kindergarten level, for instance, reading readiness experiences provide important preparation for the more structured work in reading.[14]

Pictures may be used in many ways to develop the child's ability to express his thoughts in sentences. A variety of colorful pictures that depict one action, such as a baby playing with a ball or a boy skating, may be used first. As the children are guided to think of the most important word (the subject) first, then the action word, they may be encouraged to say, "The baby is playing" rather than merely "A baby." A sentence stating that the boy is skating will be given concerning the other picture. Children who are delayed in the readiness skills will need much slowly paced help in this way, but time spent for this is worthwhile.

Games such as this one involving dramatizations may be played to create interesting activities for offering needed repetition: A child may hold up a picture in which action is obvious. He may say, "I want to do what this boy is doing. What must I do?" Another child says, "You will skate." "What do I need to do this?" "You need skates." "Where will I be when I skate?" "You will be on the sidewalk outdoors." Simple repetitive games such as this which permit the child to dramatize and express sentences will help the slower learner to develop awareness of what is meant by a sentence.

Picture dramatizations may be planned for which committees of children are assigned to be responsible for equipment or needed properties. Others may bring or prepare simple stage equipment to be used for such scenes as "outdoors," "home," "in the kitchen," and others that will add interest to the picture dramatizations.

---

[14]From Harold G. Shane, June Mulry, Mary E. Reddin, and Margaret C. Gillespie: *Improving Language Arts Instruction in the Elementary School.* 1962, pp. 11-12. Courtesy of Charles E. Merrill Books, Inc.

Classification

It is important for the children to learn to place pictures or objects in groups according to their categorical classifications, and be able to tell in their own words why they should be classified in this manner. These categories may concern size, what things are made of, people and their occupations, clothing, food, animals, seasonal groupings, and many others.

The children may begin classification with toys or real objects that are available in the home or school. They may place the things that are for work or play in their proper groups. Pasting and cutting activities may accompany the classification after the children have had sufficient practice with the three-dimensional objects.

The slower learners need much practice with simple classification, such as:

(a) "Let's name all of the big toys in this box."
(b) "Find as many blue things in the room as you can."
(c) "Name some people who are wearing long sleeves today."

Even though some children are able to readily classify several related or similar pictured objects, such as choosing a bus and train when asked to tell which are associated with a car from a series, or indicating two kinds of fruit that belong with a certain type of fruit within another grouping, the students may still be limited in their ability to describe or tell reasons why some things belong together in a series. A group of first graders were viewing filmstrip picture series for the purpose of describing possible classifications. When asked, "Which belong together?" many children could not generalize or express broad conclusions. They possessed few individual ideas or unique observations to be shared and discussed with their classmates. Their teacher provided supplementary experiences in which the children were able to describe, classify, explain reasons for the relationships of pictured objects, and tell why some things did not belong, and to repeat this practice in a variety of similar settings. The child who has command of observational and associational skills can freely express numerous ways in which he sees why some things may be classified together or why others do not belong. To do this, the child must have at his command a sufficient background of experience. This ability is preparatory to creative and analytical reading. How much of himself, his own ideas, observations or experiences a child can put into his reading makes a difference in the caliber of his comprehension and ability to apply what he reads.

Interpretation and Identification of Emotions

Learning to determine how a picture or story character feels according to his facial expressions or actions is necessary to prepare the child for later interpreting the feelings of characters in reading content. The reader must interpret word stories or descriptions and understand the emotional reactions of the characters, how their feelings, thoughts or actions may be influenced by events in the story and be able to carry these observations over into critical and analytical aspects of reading.

Capable and critical readers can become aware of the needs of society as described in books, newspaper events and editorials. The thoughtful and purposeful reader may gain the awareness of himself as one who shares the responsibilities with others for meeting social needs. Such preparation has its roots in the readiness stage and does not just suddenly burst into bloom all at once when the student enters a high school or college current events or social studies class.

A teacher of a first-grade class read the story of the ant and the grasshopper to the students. The story unfolded with the described industrious work of the ant and climaxed with the helpless plight of the indolent grasshopper when the ant refused to give him food in the freezing winter.

"What do you think?" asked the teacher at the close of the story. "Do you think that the grasshopper should have worked harder and planned a way to take care of himself?"

"Some people can't," replied thoughtful little Jody. Her teacher listened and waited for her to continue.

The child went on, "Johnny's mother tells him to fix his breakfast each morning, but he can't take care of himself very well, so I asked him to stop at my house and I fix his breakfast." Both were children whose parents worked and left the house very early each day.

The teacher explained how the animal-talking fables are often intended to teach a lesson, but she also expressed appreciation of the child's thoughtful criticism and application of this one's events to an emotional and social need shared by all people: the need to be helped and to be able to help.

The children who cannot reach the level of critical and interpretative reading also need to be able to understand some of the emotional reactions and feelings of story characters. This helps them to "live with" Wild West Joe and his adventures or share experiences with other favorite characters in books containing easy vocabulary but high interest appeal. Enjoyment of television or movies involves interpretation of emotional reactions by the viewer. The listeners worriedly and tensely "sit on the edges of their seats" as they vicariously prevent the crooks from cheating their intended victim and seizing his ranch or ride with the cavalry troops who arrive just in the nick of time to help the few heroic soldiers who are managing to hold down the fort though far outnumbered.

Learning To Call Up and Talk About Sensory Images

Children need help with learning to describe their sensory images of how things taste, feel or sound as they interpret pictured meanings, word pictures and descriptions in their reading. The use of sensory images as aids to reading is dependent upon a rich background of sensory and other experiences.

Sufficient time should be permitted for the children to experience, to the greatest possible extent, the sensory aspects of stories that are read to them or presented by the use of filmstrips and other media. Slower learners need a variety of ways to share, hear and feel the experiences that are being described in the story. The story of *The Three Bears* which can be read to the students from a story book or filmstrip, offers a variety of sensory images, their lively descriptions and comparisons. Papa Bear's porridge was too *hot;* Mama's was too *cold*. The beds were either too *hard* or too *soft*. Rather than merely reading, "Papa's porridge was too hot," much pupil participation should be encouraged as each sensory image is described. (Shivering when *cold* is mentioned, blowing burned fingers and puckering up feignedly burned mouths, and observations and descriptions of pictured details, such as steam coming from the porridge bowl are all good.) Sensory images really can stimulate the imagination and inspire both teacher and pupil to really "go creative" and not hesitate to "ham it up" to enjoy the story to the utmost. The "too high" or "too low" chairs may be prepared especially for the children to easily visualize the small, middle-sized and large sizes as they listen. Enthusiastic children are easily encouraged to use the imagination and the advantage of whatever is available for use in re-creating these listening-dramatization story situations.

Many follow-up activities are possible after each presentation of sensory words. The students may bring pictures that portray the new sensory words that have been added to their sensory conceptual vocabulary. The pictures may show action, hot, cold, and many other new meanings. Questions may be asked to motivate the child to think about the sensory images, noises or actions suggested by what is happening in the pictures. The children may be encouraged to draw pictures to illustrate abstract sensory meanings, such as "swish," "something soft," etc.

Children in a class for trainable mentally handicapped were asked to dramatize their sensory images as the teacher said "key" words. The following dramatized actions were given by a child as the key words were said.

Key Word	Pretended Actions
(a) Eating	Put on salt and pepper, ate and drank, and made sounds of drinking and swallowing.
(b) Hot	Flattened and patted a hamburger in his hand and then fried it.
(c) Cold	Cleaned off the windshield and started the car. He made the sound of the car.

Children may imitate the sounds or actions suggested to them by listening to music or story records.

Auditory Readiness

Ability to distinguish differences in sounds may be devoloped by first learning to give very basic responses to sounds. Children may be asked to listen as noises are produced by toys selected from a small group, then they may indicate which of the toys made each sound. This game may be played as follows:

The teacher may instruct the children to listen carefully as the noise from each toy is demonstrated, then the group of toys will be left in view of the children. A duplicate set of similar toys may be hidden behind a screen. As a toy from the hidden group is caused to produce a sound, the children may take turns indicating by pointing or telling which toy from the group is like the one that made the noise.

Recordings or animal sounds may be prepared through the use of a tape recorder. As each animal sound is introduced, a picture of the animal may be shown to the children. All of the pictures may then be arranged on the bulletin board in the room. As the taped sounds are presented, the children may point, tell or dramatize to indicate which animal made each sound. A small transistor tape recorder may be used to record sounds of the animals at the farm, county or state fairs, or wherever a variety of animals may be available. Pictures or slides of the animals may be used with the sound taped recordings.

Record series of familiar sounds are available for auditory skill instruction. They may include sounds in the home, on the farm, trains and other locomotion sounds. The children may listen and dramatize their impressions or imitate certain sounds and identify them.

The Ginn Manual for *Building Pre-reading Skills, Kit A* contains an activity for classification of objects according to sound. The children begin by describing sounds to accompany pictured objects that are placed in their card holder. They are encouraged and helped to describe the sounds that the objects would make, using descriptive words such as *loud, soft, low, high, sharp, exciting,* and *pretty*. They discuss where the sounds might be heard: at home, at school, or outdoors.

> Remove the cards from the card holder and give each one to a child. Ask, 'Who has something that we could probably hear outdoors?' When a suitable object has been suggested, have the child place the card in the upper left pocket of the card holder. Continue in a similar manner, having a child place a card for the other two categories, *Sounds Heard at School* and *Sounds Heard at Home*. Help the children classify the remaining nine

pictures in the appropriate categories. The final arrangement would be similar to the following:

(Sounds Heard Outdoors)	(Sounds Heard at School)	((Sounds Heard at Home)
fire engine	ball bouncing	vacuum cleaner
jet plane	hammer	tea kettle
lawn mower	saw	food mixer
	bird	telephone
		clock

Some illustrations may be placed in more than one category. The bird, for instance, might be heard at home or at school. When all twelve pictures have been placed, review with the children the three catgories and the pictures in each one.

Mature children may be able to classify the sounds according to place very rapidly. They might then classify the pictures under other headings such as *loud sounds, soft sounds, high sounds, low sounds.*[15]

Children need help in listening to all of the syllables in words. When the students in a class for trainable retarded were asked to point to pictured objects as the teacher named them, several children confused "thimble" and "needle" apparently because they heard only the last syllable. They had previous experiences to help them to be familiar with a needle, but some whose mothers did not use a thimble still pointed to it when "needle" was pronounced.

These children had difficulty with learning to say words of more than one syllable. Other students confused "jacks" and "jacket," "lion" and "wheel" and "whale," and yet they were familiar with these pictures and their word meanings. The lack of auditory discrimination apparently caused their difficulties.

The use of these abilities should be emphasized in activities during the pre-reading period. The children may be introduced to such skills through use of pre-reading techniques and instructional aids. Although they are not, at this time, working with a sight vocabulary or other formal reading materials they are gaining a background of experiences to help in their preparation for reading skills. They can, for example, through the use of pictures, begin to interpret meanings, present their observations, and organize ideas. Sufficient mastery of many such basic skills can be gained before the additional complex formal reading vocabulary and its use are also introduced.

---

[15]Clymer, Christenson, and Russsell: *Manual for Building Pre-reading Skills, Kit A, Language. loc. Cit.,* pp. 71-2.

The child who is delayed in the basic pre-reading skills cannot handle too many new areas that seem to demand his mastery simultaneously.

The children need much practice in problem-solving, making evaluations, organizing and other uses of the higher thought processes long before they begin formal reading. Too many complex skills are often introduced to children before they have had sufficient opportunities to really acquire each one. The step-by-step building upon that which has been previously established is well worth the time and effort needed, and pays off in pupil reading success. The gifted reader seemingly masters these skills without very much detailed developmental introduction, but if the slower learners have a shaky foundation in any one important pre-reading area, there is soon an accumulation of reading troubles confronting the children and endangering their self-confidence, which in turn also adds to their learning handicaps.

Examples of ways in which the higher thought processes can be developed through pre-reading activities follow.

1. *Retelling a Sequence of Events*

After a trip to the zoo, several activities may be listed on the experience chart during class discussion period, such as:

We went to see the lions.

We saw some funny monkeys.

We bought tickets at the gate.

The children may be asked to tell the order in which all of these things happened, or they may be asked to answer such questions as, "Did we see the lions before we saw the monkeys?" "What did we have to do before we could get into the zoo?"

Another group of things that occurred could be listed on the chart, such as:

A parrot said, "Shut up!"

A man was cleaning the elephant's house.

A monkey scratched his ear.

The guide told us about the animals.

A monkey rode a tricycle.

The children may be asked to name the funny things that happened.

They may answer such thought questions as:

"Let's name three animals and try to think of the things that the guide told us about them."

"What funny thing did one monkey do just before the other one rode the tricycle?"

"What did we see that helped us to know that many people must work to make the zoo a nice place to visit?"

Picture Observations: Pictures that depict an event that has just happened, such as a little boy with paint spilled on himself may be shown to the children. Questions that require noting and describing the preceding incident may be asked, such as:

"Why does the little boy have paint all over his hands?"

"Tell the story that you think may have caused something to happen."

"What do you think Mother will do when she finds out?"

"What season is it? How do you know that it is winter?"

Many interesting pictures can be obtained from magazines, calendars and other sources for this activity.

Teachers of first grade emphasize the need for some students to be provided with sufficient experiences to develop independent work habits. The extremely short attention and interest span of some beginners prevents them from staying with a task until they complete it. They lack the self-confidence necessary for working independently or quietly enough to permit others to work unhindered.

Some children have problems relating to their lack of ability to choose activities or use their leisure or free time to their advantage when they are given the opportunity for this type of choice. These children need much help during the readiness stage of their reading program to enable them to make choices, develop self-directional ability and to gain both competence and self-confidence.

More teacher devised instructional materials are needed for use in the readiness areas. The children are intrigued by a variety of interesting materials to manipulate, handle, and move. Too much dependence upon commercially prepared instructional aids cannot fulfill all of the needs. The children are as interested in working with materials prepared from scrap items that may be available in the home as they are in using the commercially designed instructional aids so abundantly available today through many sources to the school and parents.

Too many activities requiring the use of merely workbooks and paper seatwork cannot provide sufficiently for manipulative and eye-hand coordination skills. Some children need so much additional practice to further this growth. Short attention and interest spans can be increased through pupil participation in tasks involving the use of a variety of materials. A child who is bored by looking at rows of flat pictures will have his enthusiasm renewed by a row of small toys or other three dimensional objects for use in indicating likenesses and differences or performance of some other skill-building activity.

Many workbooks progress too quickly from the very easy to the more difficult in skill area introduction. Although this introduction of skills is paced in accordance with the abilities of most students, the slower learner needs much supplementary help and additional repetition in the areas of his difficulty. This student usually needs much more repetition of some of the same skills, but this must be provided in a variety of interesting settings. The accompanying manuals often suggest a variety of additional supplementary activities that are helpful, but it may be more meaningful if a broader background of experiences could be provided for the student in some of the subskills previous to the introduction of the workbook. Finer discrimination of words and letters in the workbook will be much easier for the child who has had much preparation through the use of the flannel board, pegboard, three-dimensional objects, and other media to indicate likenesses and differences. A rich pre-reading program that provides for the needed skills would possibly help the delayed learner who, even with the supplementary help that is given between the presentation of each skill in the new workbook lessons, still has trouble with many skills.

Teachers' manuals that accompany several basic pre-reading programs may be referred to by the teacher who is in search of help with the provision of supplementary activities to reinforce and support pupil growth in specific skill areas. Workbooks or manuals are valuable sources for the planning and preparation of instructional aids.

If, for some children, the workbook pages contain too many

items, special adaptation of the pages to the abilities of the children to cope with them may be done by cutting items from the pages and mounting them on construction paper or using them with the audiovisual equipment.

Pupil interest is especially important in the effort to help the child who is delayed in any of the skills. When the student becomes tired, he may no longer do his best, but may mark anything to finish the task. This lack of interest can be lessened through the use of a variety of materials that require different types of responses other than marking an item with a pencil or crayon.

Children need much experience in observing pictures that relate to past or anticipated holidays or seasons to help in visualizing something that has happened at a time other than the present day. A group of preschoolers were shown a Halloween pictured scene in which costumed children were going to a party. A little boy said, "They are all dressed up for Halloween, but it isn't Halloween." The teacher guided his thinking to help him to realize that although he was looking at the picture on a July afternoon, it was Halloween in the picture.

Left-to-right progression skill should be developed during the readiness period before the child is faced with the need to learn a sight vocabulary and other reading abilities. There is a mechanical skill involved in the child's learning to always start on the left side of the page, direct his view steadily across the row to the right, return to the left side and continue viewing each row in succession. Mastery of this skill can be accomplished before he must also be concerned with interpretation of the printed symbols in addition to the left-to-right progression of rows.

Activities to help the child to understand the concept of a "row" should be first introduced before the complete left-to-right sweep is expected. Activities to promote this understanding are as follows:

1. **Use of large charts with pictures** in rows that are numbered. The teacher may direct the children to name the things in row two, etc.

The children may be directed to count the things in certain rows.

They may answer questions pertaining to the rows. "What

row has the picture of the wagon?" "Look at the row that has the boat. Tell what picture comes next in line after the boat."
2. Two or three rows of narrow colored tape may be placed across a sheet of paper. Wide spaces may be left between the rows of tape. Dots may be marked on the tape with a felt pen. The children may be directed to start from the left each time and paste a picture on each dot. They may learn to build rows in this manner.
3. Various colored construction paper circles, squares, etc. may be pasted in rows on a large chart, each row being numbered. The children may name the colors for each row. Seatwork in which they paste things in rows may be done.

There is a need for the children to be able to use the meanings of place *relationships* in as many practical situations as possible. This can be done through interesting and varied activities in which they listen for the directions of the teacher or parent and follow them as they understand the meanings of new words concerning place relationships. They may follow such directions as:

1. "Let's put the toys away and put all of the trains and trucks on the **top** shelf."
2. "Let's put the **biggest** toys on the **bottom** shelf."
3. They may place felt figures on the **left** or **right** side of the flannel board as directed. The flannel board may also be used for placing objects **up** or **down;** at the **top** or **bottom.** A felt strip or narrow line may be placed in the middle or at another designated place on the board. The children may place felt figures **above** or **below** the line.

These activities help the pre-readers to understand and visualize the meaning of *place* and its relationship. This repeated use and application of the place names to their meanings will help to provide the needed pupil vocabulary and conceptual background.

Orientation

The Ginn pre-reading program stresses the importance of a proper orientation and introduction to the skills.

Research and classroom practice have amply demonstrated that a proper orientation and introduction to the skills necessary for success in the early stages of reading can be attained by a carefully planned pre-reading program. Although some children may learn to read successfully without such a program, nearly all children will achieve this goal more readily if the school has provided good instruction in the crucial pre-reading skills.

General objectives of the Ginn pre-reading program are for providing experiences which build the foundation of skills necessary to a successful beginning in reading without actual participation in the reading of the printed symbol. The activities in the lessons in the Language Kit A are designed to help the child acquire skills in six basic areas of learning. The skills, listed by areas, follow.

Thinking

1. Recognizing and identifying pictured objects.
2. Observing and interpreting picture details.
3. Clarifying concepts.
4. Relating personal experiences to vicarious experiences.
5. Interpreting and discussing a story, a poem, or a nursery rhyme.
6. Interpreting feelings and emotions.
7. Understanding a story problem.
8. Recognizing and recalling a sequence of events.
9. Placing a series of pictures in the correct sequence from left to right.
10. Grasping the main idea.
11. Classifying
12. Generalizing about picture details.
13. Making inferences.
14. Using relationships as an aid to memory.
15. Distinguishing between make-believe and reality.
16. Predicting outcomes.
17. Making comparisons.
18. Drawing conclusions·
19. Summarizing information.
20. Perceiving relationships among mother and baby animals.

---

[16]Clymer, Christenson, and Russell: *Manual for Building Pre-reading Skills, Kit A,* Language, Ibid., p. 1.

Oral Language Growth

1. Creating oral text for a picture story.
2. Expressing ideas in complete sentences.
3. Extending word usage and increasing speaking vocabulary.
4. Using appropriate words to describe emotions, feelings, actions, and sensory images.
5. Dictating ideas in an organized way for an experience chart.
6. Discussing a story, a poem, or a nursery rhyme.
7. Clarifying word meanings.

Listening

1. Listening to and enjoying poems.
2. Listening to and enjoying nursery rhymes.
3. Listening to and enjoying a story.
4. Listening to and appreciating the contributions of others.
5. Listening to and following directions.

Visual Discrimination

1. Detecting likenesses and differences.
2. Relating a single pictured object to a similar object in a large scene.
3. Identifying colors.

Auditory Perception

1. Identifying and discriminating among sounds in the environment.
2. Identifying and imitating animal sounds.
3. Recognizing and supplying rhyming words.

Directional Orientation

1. Perceiving and describing space relationships and using the terms top-middle-bottom, above-below, over-on-under, up-down, beside-between, in front of-behind, and left-right.
2. Understanding the relationship between size and distance.
3. Moving eyes from left to right.
4. Observing a series of pictures from left to right.[17]

---

[17]Clymer, Christenson, and Russell: *Manual for Building Pre-reading Skills,* Kit A, Language, Ibid., pp. 10-12.

Objectives of Kit B—Building Pre-reading Skills

The Kit B program provides experiences which build a foundation of skills necessary to a rapid and successful beginning in reading. The primary focus is on the use of context and knowledge of initial consonants as an aid to word recognition. The main objectives of Kit B are as follows:

1. To teach the use of context for anticipation of appropriate response.
2. To teach the terms "alike," "different," and "beginning sound."
3. To develop auditory perception of beginning sounds in words.
4. To develop association of initial consonant sounds with the letters which represent them.
5. To teach the letter names and the upper and lower-case forms of fifteen consonants.

In addition to lessons carefully formulated to develop these five objectives, optional lessons are provided which develop language skills through a more or less informal program of language activities.[18]

Mrs. Roberta Johnson, a teacher of first grade at Maplewood School in Garden City, Michigan, stressed the need for children to have specific pre-reading help for the following:

1. **Learning To Listen and Share the Turns To Talk.** Children need the opportunities to take time to express themselves and the reassurance that their classmates will wait and listen to their contributions. They must have time to think, to try, and to know that their efforts are considered important enough to be permitted this needed time. Teachers need to remember that the **child** of whom the question is being asked is more important than the answer in itself, and a child should be given sufficient time to think, organize his thoughts, and to seek answers. A too-hasty going-on to call upon another student if the answer is not immediately forthcoming from one child can sometimes penalize the thoughtful child who may be carefully thinking his answer

---

[18]Clymer, Theodore, Christenson, Bernice M., and Russell, David H.: *Manual for Building Pre-reading Skills,* Kit B, 1965. Published by Ginn and Company, Boston, Mass. Used with permission.

through before expressing it. The other students will readily respect the rights of individuals in this way and will be willing to wait if they are encouraged to do so.

2. **Following directions** after first carefully listening to fully understand what is expected.

3. **Learing To Utilize Time Well.** Mrs. Johnson described a definite lack of student ability shown in many activities involving general skills that are necessary for group or independent work.

Ability To See Likenesses and Differences

Children must have ample opportunity to master the skill of discrimination of differences in objects, pictures, and shapes involving plain form as well as bright colors before they are expected to see likenesses and differences in words. Matching likenesses and indicating differences involves needed readiness to prepare the reader for noting parts of some words that are alike and the areas of their differences. This is another key skill that can be utilized by the student in the complex process of reading, and it offers a needed contribution to his reading success.

1. *Gross Discrimination Skills:* Ability to indicate likenesses and differences in size, color and position of large three dimensional objects, felt figures, and pictures.

2. *Finer Discrimination:* Ability to match likenesses and indicate differences in smaller shapes, large and small sized capital letters, lower-case letters, and words.

Other pre-reading skills presented in the audio-visual section, and some of the areas included here are also described in more detail with suggested activities for their development.

Internal Detail

Ability to distinguish finer likenesses and differences in internal detail is a complex skill necessary to success in reading. This enables the reader to distinguish between longer words that are similar, and is helpful as the child's reading vocabulary becomes larger and he is expected to use reading as a tool.

Internal detail at the pre-reading level involves a series of pictured objects in which a part within one is different from the others. Differences may be found in one small portion of one of the objects, such as a picture of three or four kings wearing crowns. The crown of one may be different in a minute detail. The child must be able to locate the different one and its area of difference.

Internal differences may involve a part missing from one pictured object, such as four ducks, each with an umbrella, but the handle is missing from one duck's umbrella.

The child must also be able to find what is wrong from a pattern of internal detail, as in four pictured baskets of fruit with an apple missing from one. Since the other three baskets contain the apple in that location, the child must scrutinize and compare them to determine what is wrong or how one differs in comparison with the others.

Varied Detail

This readiness skill helps to prepare the child for later discrimination ability in reading, making general comparisons, critical evaluation of reading content and drawing conclusions.

Varied detail is used to determine differences in pictured objects all of which are different, but one is most different. Such picture series as four windows, all decorated differently, but one is rounded at the top while the others are all square, serve as an example. The children may observe and discuss the general differences and likenesses and make the decision concerning which is most different in the characteristics of varied detail.

Plastic "take-apart" toys may be used to give supplementary practice in discrimination of internal and varied detail. Three duplicate sets may make it possible to have three toys that are the same, but a detailed part may be removed from one. *Example*: Three clowns with the hat missing from one.

A source for obtaining a series of such toys is listed in the Appendix.

Directional Differences

This involves discrimination of differences in position and direction. There may be four pictures of ducks three facing the left, one looking right. Mastery of this skill helps the child to quickly note likenesses and differences in words that are similar except at the beginning or end. Such word differences as *there* and *where, when* and *where, stop* and *spot,* and others will possibly not cause the reader as much difficulty if he has had the benefit of much readiness preparation for determining directional differences.

A prolonged readiness preparation in discrimination of likenesses and differences in internal and varied detail and directional differences will possibly help to prepare the child to read more carefully and not to hastily substitute words as he reads.

"Read what is there," the child often is reminded, although to his knowledge, he is reading what he sees. He has apparently not mastered the skill of quickly distinguishing the differences in words according to the above described characteristics.

Pre-reading activities to aid in the development of discrimination of likenesses and differences in these areas are as follows.

1. Use of pictures or filmstrips to provide additional practice in indicating these differences.

2. Preparation of series for use with overhead and opaque projectors.

3. Three-dimensional objects placed on the child's desk, and felt items for use on the flannel board.

4. Take apart plastic toys from one of which a minute detail may be removed for the child to find and indicate as different.

5. Picture series drawn by the children which they can share with each other during class activities for the development of this skill.

Serial Order

The competent reader must be able to note and remember likenesses and differences and positions of things in one series and their relationships to other series. This enables him to apply this to likenesses, differences and positions of letters in one word as compared with another. Knowledge of serial order is applied to words that are similar, and this is one skill that is used to not confuse the many similar words as one reads. Such words as "how" and "who" that contain the same letters which are different in position are rapidly distinguished and identified even though the reader may not be aware that he is doing such discrimination of the words.

Pre-reading activities to develop skill in distinguishing serial order may be listed.

1. Matching rows of pictures or shapes from the left side of a page or side of the flannel board or chalkboard to their corresponding rows on the right side. Three or four shapes or pictures may be used, but arranged differently for each row. Children need much practice and repetition to develop this skill. If they cannot match likenesses in serial order involving gross shapes or pictures, they will be very confused when confronted with words in this manner.

2. Seatwork activities for which they draw lines to match likenesses in serial order or duplicate patterns or rows.

    (a) The teacher may draw two or three rows of shapes on the board, such as a circle, square and a triangle; a triangle, square and another triangle, etc. The children may arrange construction paper shapes in rows to match these patterns to be pasted on their papers.

    (b) The children may take turns putting a pattern on the board. They may call on a classmate to duplicate each pattern, either directly under it or on the opposite side.

The Eye-Gate House filmstrip, although especially prepared for auditory discrimination,[19] may be used also to develop skill in distinguishing serial order in letters. A series of letters are grouped in sections as follows:

MM	WW	SS	EE
MW	MM	HA	SS

The child may be directed to find the sections that are alike, and to do this he must learn to look carefully at both letters in the grouping.

Mastery of the ability to distinguish likenesses in groupings of two letters leads to the attack of three—letter series.

MWM	WMW

MWM

This ability to distinguish likenesses when viewing two or three letter series must be mastered before the additional requirement of remembering word symbols is involved.

Listening Skills for Reading Readiness

Listening is a skill with which children need help. They cannot

---

[19]Eye-Gate Filmstrip 85 B, *Auditory Discrimination*. Courtesy of Eye-Gate House, Inc.

be expected to acquire this skill unaided, because there must be a clearly understood goal shared by both learner and instructor if the learning through listening experience is to be most effective. This goal or purpose for listening helps the learner to choose and distinguish accurately the important or purposeful and set it apart to be remembered, evaluated, and heeded as directions are followed or assignments completed.

> Just as there is a sequence of the skills involved in speaking, there is a sequence in the growth pattern of listening skills. Provision should be made for active participation in experiences which require the child to listen for specific purposes in all areas of the daily program.[20]

An accusing "You're not listening!" can be as harmful as saying to a child whose arithmetic problems are incorrect, "Your work is not correct," without providing the necessary help in guiding the student to correct the mathematical errors. Both students' problems are equally indicative of a need for help.

Classroom situations in which teacher and students share purposeful listening activities are especially meaningful.

Special emphasis upon the importance of each student's verbal contributions and the encouragement of others to listen will not only improve listening ability in the class, but will help the attention and interest span to grow. This will also permit growth by the slower learner whose self-confidence may just bloom as his classmates attentively listen to *his* ideas or care enough to be interested in what *he* thinks about a subject.

Discussion activities are helpful in which it is clearly emphasized that there is no "right" or "wrong" answers, but "Let's think about it and share our ideas." "Let's listen as Bill tells why he thinks everybody should play safely on the playground," etc., and other discussions will encourage pupil participation because they need not fear being wrong.

Discussions to encourage purposeful listening may involve these topics:

1. Safety, health, good citizenship and other rules.

---

[20]Clymer, Christenson, and Russell: Manual for *Building Pre-reading Skills, Kit A,* Language, *loc. cit.,* p. 15.

2. Picture study and discussion. Filmstrips and slides may be used for this activity, also. The pupil interest is very keen during activities in which the projectors are used. Children also enjoy observing and telling details that they think are important, telling what could be possible through the use of their imaginations and drawing from their own interest and experiential backgrounds for the sharing and discussion. Stressing the fact that the better the children listen, the more time is available for turns to talk also encourages good listening.

3. *The tape recorder* can be used for listening in a variety of ways. Recordings may be made of animal sounds, those made by toys, etc. Children may be instructed to listen for various purposes, such as:

"Listen to see how many kinds of animal sounds you can hear. Be ready to name some of them later."

"Listen to these toys make noise. Try to remember which ones made the *loudest* noises. Remember this so that you can name them to us." Listening activities are possible through the use of the tape recorder to permit pupil participation as they listen. Word or sound series in which three sounds are alike and one is different may be prepared for use. The children may be directed to listen and raise their hands when they hear the different sound or word. As they listen to recorded nursery rhymes, they may prepare to name the words that rhyme. *Loud* and *soft* sounds may be recorded. They may be instructed to raise their left hands for the loud sounds and their right hands for the soft ones.

4. *Auditory discrimination filmstrips* which are available from Eye-Gate House, Inc., contain pictures in color that begin with the initial consonants. The children may name the pictures and tell which begin alike or which one is different in the beginning sound. These may be used for listening skills as well as the development of the auditory discrimination skill. Filmstrips that involve the naming of rhyming words may be used for listening, too.

5. *The opaque projector* may be used with small pictures cut from old workbooks, magazines, catalogs, etc. Such directions for listening may be given as:

"Listen and see how many animals John can name."

"Let's listen as Jim names these pictures. Remember to raise your hand when he names a picture of some kind of fruit" (or toy, tool for work, etc.).

6. Projection transparencies may be purchased or prepared for use with the *overhead projector*. They may involve pictures for naming and listening for specified reasons:

"Listen as Sally names a picture. She will then call on someone."

Children may be called upon to tell something about a certain projected picture then call upon someone else to find and point to it. They may be warned that there will be no repeating of the descriptions, so if they want a turn in this listening game, they must keep their ears tuned in to listen.

7. A variety of felt objects may be placed on the *flannel board*. Children may take turns describing a felt object and calling upon someone to find and indicate the described object.

This same listening game may be played with the use of the *Hook N' Loop Board,* which provides for the use of three-dimensional objects.

8. Felt figures of various colors may be placed on the flannel board. A child may take a turn finding an object on the board and describing its color, then telling who may be wearing an article of clothing that is the same color. The child may say, "Here is a green pear. It is the same color as Joe's shirt." If Joe is listening carefully, he then may have a turn. If he does not hear, he forfeits his turn, and someone else who was able to identify the described article of clothing may have the turn.

Musical games or songs in which the children must listen and perform a specified activity at a particular time are very helpful to teach listening as well as other skills.

This song and art lesson may be correlated for the purpose of helping the children learn to listen as well as the other instructional aim of teaching the relationship of parts to wholes. A large construction paper pumpkin may be used with the facial features cut out separately to be pinned or pasted in place as the following song is sung by the class:

My Jack-o-lantern
Oh, once I had a pumpkin,
A pumpkin—a pumpkin—
Oh, once I had a pumpkin—

With no face at all.
With no eyes
And no nose
And no mouth
And no teeth
Oh, once I had a pumpkin
With no face at all.
So I made a jack-o-lantern
Jack-o-lantern—jack-o-lantern
So I made a jack-o-lantern
With a big funny face.
With big eyes
And big nose
And big mouth
And big teeth
So I made a jack-o-lantern
With a big funny face. [21]

The song, "Little Sir Echo"[22] may be used for listening and ringing bells, too. The children may sing this song and listen for the echo after each "Hello" and let their bells be the echo. The frequent repetition of this echo will permit the children to *listen* and *do* for a sufficient time to really help in the building of listening skills.

Listening, singing and being prepared to clap hands at a certain place in songs are activities that are favorites with children.

Rhythm records for primary children involve listening and action combined. One that contains both reading and arithmetic readiness activities is available from Rhythm Record Company and also distributed by the F. A. Owen Publishing Company. This series is presented in the appendix.

Parents can do much to help their children to develop good listening skills through the provision of interesting trips and excursions. Sources of interest that are available in most communi-

[21]From *Ginn Music News,* Fall, 1964. Published by Ginn and Company. Used with permission.
Ardith Shelley: *My Jack-o-lantern,* p. 8.
(To be sung to tune, "Did You Ever See A Lassie?")
[22]From Lorraine E. Watters, Louis Wersen, Willeam Hartshorn, L. Eileen McMillan, Alice Gallup: *The Magic of Music,* Book 1, 1965, pp. 14-15. Courtesy of Ginn and Company.

ties are included. Parents and teachers may make it possible for the children to visit at least the places of interest that are easy to reach within the community.[23]

Airports	Bridges	City-county buildings	
Dairies	Parks	Coca Cola®Bottling Companies	
Children's museums		Edison Company	
Nature Trails		Aquariums	Art museums
Puppet theatres		Libraries	Farmers' markets
Federal buildings		Potato chip factories	
Automotive buildings		Goodwill industries	
Street railways		Vernor's® Ginger Ale Companies	
Young people's concerts		Pet shops	City hall
Nurseries		Police and fire departments	
Post Office		Greenhouses	National banks
Telephone company		Bird sanctuaries	
Radio and TV stations		Newspaper office	
Railroad stations			

This prepared booklet was provided by the Maplewood Parent-teachers' Association for use by parents in planning experiential trips with their children during the summer and other recreational time. Many of the suggested sources are utilized by teachers in planning field trips in correlation with special class unit studies. Purposeful listening can be easily motivated and continued through such direct experiences.

Shane and his co-authors define three levels of listening and observing ability through which children progress.

The power to listen develops through analogous levels at which a child can (1) **identify** a sound (for example, an automobile horn), (2) **interpret** the sound (an auto horn as distinct from the more feeble honk of a bicycle horn), and (3) **describe** the sound (as a honk, beep, musical tone, etc.)[24]

These levels should be provided for as the child is taught to listen, and the developmental aspect of this skill of listening is as necessary as the sequential skill development in any other learning area. Provision for the child to learn to listen enables him to more

---

[23]A list was prepared to include specific names of sources in the Detroit and suburban areas, but some general ones have been included for any community. From *Community Classroom* 1963 compiled and prepared by the Parent-teachers Association of Maplewood School, Garden City, Michigan.

[24]Harold G. Shane, June Grant Mulry, Mary E. Reddin, and Margaret C. Gillespie, *loc. cit.*, p. 114.

fully use this valuable skill as a tool to aid in learning and appreciation. The child who learns to listen can more purposefully listen to learn.

Chapter VII

READINESS ACTIVITIES FOR PRE-READERS

I NSTRUCTIONAL DEVICES and materials prepared by the author to develop language skills, eye-hand coordination and other skills were used with a class of trainable retarded children and also were used in a kindergarten class by a teacher at Maplewood School in Garden City, Michigan. The purpose was to evaluate the materials and attempt to determine whether they would be helpful in identifying and providing for some of the readiness skills lacked by the slower learners in the kindergarten class.

Some of the mentally retarded students in the trainable class became very skillful in certain activities. A few of the students who were in the fifty IQ-test-score range achieved some success in certain readiness areas according to some of the standardized reading readiness test results after two years of readiness preparation, repetition and reinforcement in needed skill areas.

This motivated the author and the teacher of the kindergarten class to seek to determine whether or not other children who have not achieved success in the readiness areas could possibly benefit from such materials and techniques used to develop their needed skills. Would not a prolonged readiness period that allowed for needed reinforcement, repetition and remedial instruction at each skill level needed by the student prevent many of the later reading failures?

The activities were started in March, 1965, and involved the use of the prepared instructional materials with the kindergarten children. The students were permitted to choose the materials with which they wished to work during their daily free-choice activity periods. They were given the choice regarding use of these materials or other things in the room to be used during free activity periods. The enthusiasm and interest were keen.

Although the purpose for the use of the materials was to determine their validity in helping the slower students, the faster, average and slower learners all enjoyed participating in the activities.

When the teacher of the kindergartners evaluated the instructional aids, she found that some would be more helpful at the beginning of the kindergarten year while others were recommended for use during the latter part of the second semester. Some activities were recommended as testing devices to be used in evaluating pupil growth in pre-reading skill areas.

An evaluation sheet was prepared to include criteria for determining educational values and student reactions to each of the instructional devices. The kindergarten teacher recorded the student responses and listed other observations that were considered pertinent.

The described materials, the student reactions, and the teacher evaluation of them are included for the purpose of sharing them with other teachers of pre-reading students.

Teacher Evaluation of Learning Devices

Device ....

Readiness Area ....

Purpose ....

Evaluation Criteria

Instructional Values	**Rating**		
	Positive	Fair	Poor
1. Appearance			
2. Purpose			
3. Provision for Growth			
4. Interesting			
5. Clear Directions			
6. Easy but Valuable			
7. Meets individual needs			
8. Sufficiently challenging			

Student Reactions
1. Interested
2. Completion of Activity
3. Learning new skills
4. Carry-over to other activities

5. Change in behavior
6. Change in abilities

Teacher Evaluation of Learning Devices

Device ....

Readiness Area ....

Purpose ....

Teacher's Comments

1. Do you think that this device provides for growth in the readiness area involved?

2. Does this device cause growth in skills that are purposeful to the children in other skill areas? (Is the child now more confident, able to assume responsibilities, use his free time constructively, etc.?)

3. Has this device caused change in behavior or pupil attitudes?

Readiness Activities, Devices, and Techniques Used with Pre-reading Students

Picture Matching Chart for Visual Perception of Likenesses in Pictures: Pictures of seals (animals, flowers, birds, etc.) were pasted individually in small squares on a tagboard chart. Small cardboard discs contained the corresponding pictures, and the children placed them in their proper places on the chart.

The kindergarten teacher observed that this activity was especially effective with the slower learners. It held their interest and gave them a feeling of achievement. They especially liked the round discs.

Tiles on Cardboard Strips for Visual Discrimination of Likenesses and Differences: Mosaic tiles of various shapes and colors were placed in rows on small cardboard strips. The children were directed to point to the one that was different in each row.

Similar strips contained three or four tiles that were the same; others were different. The children indicated those that were like the first one.

The kindergarten students were pleased with the physical arrangement of the device. The cards contained large rings, and were easy to handle and "turn the pages." The directions were simple and easy to follow.

The slower learners had difficulty with some of the items, although they could do the easier ones. This activity was recommended for use with the faster learners at the beginning of the year and for testing purposes (Fig. 1).

Figure 1. Tile strip device for likenesses and differences.

Chart Containing Rows of Small Pictured Seals to Promote Visual Discrimination of Finer Likenesses in Pictures, Likenesses in Internal Detail, and Eye-hand Coordination Skills. The children were directed to place corresponding seals contained on small cards in their proper places on the chart. This is similar to the other seal chart, but the pictures were much closer together, and were arranged in rows according to their subject categories.

The faster learners placed them exactly as they were arranged on the chart. Groups of five children worked together to complete the rows down and across. They concluded that two certain rows contained all animals and two rows were all flowers. They competed with each other as they looked at the rows and counted. They used their imaginations and added supplementary activities as they used this chart. The teacher considered this to be a good activity for the latter part of the year, because it could be used for many other purposes, such as counting, naming pictures and other culminative activities.

Pairs of Designs on large square ceramic tiles were prepared to develop visual discrimination of finer likenesses in shapes. The children were directed to place the tiles together with their corresponding designs. They grouped the tiles in twos. This activity was very popular with the kindergarten children. The tiles were easy to handle, and all of the children chose to do this activity again and again. It is a good independent activity.

This device was prepared from inch square ceramic tiles. Shapes were drawn with a felt marking pen, and two tiles were prepared to contain each design. A coat of clear lacquer preserved the design, and the children could handle the tiles.

This activity was always chosen during the free choice activity periods. Some children divided up the tiles and chose some from each other when they needed them. They counted after they had matched them. The teacher recommended this device as one to be kept available for the children to work with throughout the year (Fig. 2).

Small plastic plates and wooden beads representing all of the primary colors were used. The plates contained small circular indentions around the square bottom. Small wooden beads of the basic colors were given to the children. They were told to place beads of one color only in each plate. The beads just fitted into the round indentions.

Teacher Observations

1. The children mixed the blue and purple beads at first.

Figure   2.   Ceramic tile designs for matching.

2. The little beads were difficult to pick up quickly. This is a good activity to develop eye-hand coordination.

3. This activity is good for learning colors, and would be valuable as a beginning-of-the-year activity. It is good also for reviewing color recognition.

4. The children raced each other to see who could fill the plates first.

5. The teacher suggested placing beads of each color in individual containers for the children to choose from as they worked with their plates.

6. Comments were "This is fun!" "When can I try it?"

7. Many children watched as others worked. The faster learners could distinguish between the purple and blue, but took longer to make their selections.

This is a quiet activity. There was little conversation, but much concentration. It develops independence. Not very much teacher supervision was needed. They learned to take turns, and this activity helped to develop their self-confidence. "Can I try it again?"

Some had difficulty with orange and yellow. The procedure was easy to understand. One boy used both hands. Some children worked with three or four plates at a time.

"Our beads are bigger." They were intrigued with the fitting of the beads into the indented holes (Fig. 3).

Figure 3. Matching and grouping colored beads.

5. *A Chart Contained Rows of Small Pictured Cars.* Small cards were prepared to contain an individual car to be matched with one on the chart. This activity was planned to develop visual

discrimination of internal detail in pictures and also eye-hand co-ordination.

Teacher Observations

1. This is an activity for later in the kindergarten year.
2. This is good for helping the children learn to be aware of reversals and learning directional differences.
3. The slower children gave up when the activity was partially finished. Others voluntarily took over the task. This is a good continuous task, because the children kept going back and trying again.
4. Faster learners asked for assistance from each other. This is good for learning to give and take suggestions.
   "This is hard!"
   "I found It!"
5. Interest was renewed when the chart was placed on the floor.
6. It is better for not more than three children to work together on this at one time.
7. Some children took a car picture in their hands, moved it down along the edge until the right car was found.
8. This is a good activity to be used for children to work together and help each other (Fig. 4).

Egg carton matching devices were prepared to develop visual discrimination of finer likenesses.

Objects were placed individually in egg carton compartments. The children were given the corresponding ones to match by placing them in their proper compartments.

They were pleased with the egg cartons and the chance to work with them.

"Gee, we've got egg cartons at home!"

Devices included the following:

1. Alphabet letters to be matched in the compartments.
   The children wanted to do this at least two times before stopping. When activity time came, they said, "Can I play with these?"
   A sense of accomplishment was evident. "It only takes two minutes."
2. **Bottle caps** in egg cartons.

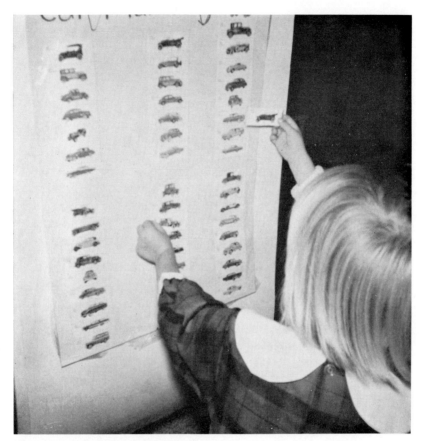

Figure 4. Matching pictures of cars.

Two people worked together.

"Can I play?"

A sense of accomplishment was evident. "We have them all right!"

This activity was preferred to the alphabet letters.

3. **Buttons** in egg cartons.

Slower learners could especially do this. This is good for learning colors and sizes.

4. **Animals** (Plastic) to be matched for likenesses.

This is good for distinguishing internal detail.

The children matched the animals on the table before putting them in the carton.

The button and animal devices were favorites of the children (Fig. 5).

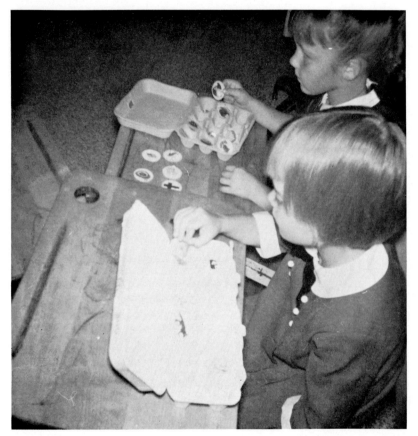

Figure 5. Egg carton matching devices.

A Fabric Matching Chart was prepared to promote visual discrimination of likenesses in internal detail and eye-hand coordination. It was planned to help retarded children learn to stay with a task, overcome their distractibility and see the activity through to completion.

Small cardboard circular tubes were covered with fabric representing various designs. Some designs were plain and others were intricate in detail. There were finer similarities in some of the fabrics. Corresponding fabric covered tubes were given to the children who were told to find and place each tube by the one like it.

The slower learners in kindergarten gave up easily. It seemed that there were too many items on the chart. Interest was not held. Faster learners could complete the chart.

The retarded children enjoyed this as a group activity. The teacher held up each tube and asked the children to look for the matching one. A few children were able to do all of them, and some loved to race with another child.

Although there was no pressure placed on the kindergarten children to complete activities, they were easily disconcerted if they had too much difficulty. The retarded children apparently felt no inward self-imposed need to accomplish this.

A large chart was prepared with fewer items, and the comment from the kindergarten was, "It's fun!"

It seems that teachers need to be aware of the self-imposed standards of children, their inner sensitivity to their failures, and to realize the need for guiding these feelings. As much guidance is needed in helping them to deal with their own self criticisms as there is needed effort to challenge them to achieve their own potential.

The second chart was much easier than the first one which contained too many items and was on a light green background. A new dark green background was much easier for the children to cope with, and they enjoyed working with this chart. It was considered important to help the children to succeed by providing the easier chart. Since the first difficult chart concerned the children, effort was made to help them to have a successful experience in this type of matching (Fig. 6).

Large pictured objects to be matched on a chart were presented for the language development skill of formulating sentences. This was found to be especially helpful during the middle of the kindergarten year (Fig. 7).

Readiness Area: Visual Discrimination to promote abilty to see differences.

Device: *Filmstrip*. The responses of the trainable and the slower kindergarten children to the items of the filmstrip were quite similar. The "trouble spots" of both groups were found in the same

Figure   6.   Matching varied detailed fabrics.

items. The kindergarten children were able to express their ideas more verbally, and there were more of them who could respond to the items.

Areas of difficulty were as listed below:

1. Items involving differences in more intricate internal detail.
2. Detailed differences in finer shapes.
3. Directional differences.
4. Reversals in position of objects. In an example in which a pumpkin was reversed, the children noted that the stem was different but they did not realize that the whole pumpkin was turned even though this was quite obvious.

In an example in which four kings wore crowns, the complete crown of one was different in shape as well as decoration, yet the children pointed out a few individual differences but could not perceive that the whole crown was different. They need help in visualizing wholes and making generalizations, such as, "The crown is different." This skill is needed as a preparation for drawing conclusions and grasping complete thoughts in reading material. Summarizing the general meanings and implications contained in content of reading material is necessary in using reading as a tool. These skills have their start in the readiness program. The way must be paved for the thinking skills needed in reading before the book is placed in the child's hand.

5. Some children had difficulty even when items were flashed

Figure 7. Matching large pictured objects.

on the screen later after the differences had been indicated previously by other children. This suggests the need for much more of this activity at a slower pace with repetition presented in a variety of interesting ways, but with the degree of difficulty paced according to the children's progress in the skill areas.

6. Many children did not use complete sentences.

Wooden forms to be placed in their outlined shapes on a chart were designed to develop visual perceptual skills, association and recognition of forms and shapes. This was for the purpose of preparing the child to see likenesses and recognize word shapes.

This quiet activity required concentration. It was very popular with all of the kindergartners. They could do it individually.

One kindergarten child could associate the feel of the forms and place them in their outlined shapes. He demonstrated this ability by reaching into the container, picking up a wooden form, and without looking at it, placing it immediately into the proper shape. Perhaps more activities involving such tactile feeling of abstract objects to be matched according to their visualized "shape" should be done in the readiness program. Such activity to promote this may be as follows:

1. Letting the child, without seeing the object hold a miniature airplane, car or other plastic toy. He may be directed to "remember how it feels." The teacher may remove the object from his hand then show him a chart containing various objects or pictures. The child may be directed to indicate which items on the chart were the same as the one that he held. After the children have thoroughly mastered the skill involving the objects or pictures on the chart, they may try to match the objects that they "felt" to stenciled items or outlined ones on a chart. This activity seems to be one that may be needed by the disadvantaged child whose experiential background is so limited. This will be described more fully in the section relating to the disadvantaged child. These children need so much help with sensory experiences.

The children performed according to their individual abilities and interests, and no two children proceeded to perform the task in the same manner (Fig 8).

Fabric Squares for Matching were arranged on a chart. The

Figure   8.   Fitting forms to outlined shapes.

chart contained eight fabrics of different colors. Corresponding sets of fabrics were glued to small cards. The children matched the fabrics by placing the small cards in their proper places on the chart.

This activity was especially good for developing the self-confidence of the slower children.

One child said, "I did it all by myself" (Fig. 9). Another chart contained basic shapes of red construction paper. The sets contained on small cards to be matched were exactly the same in shapes, but they were cut from black construction paper. The children indicated their likenesses by pointing or placing the shapes on their corresponding ones.

Figure   9.   Matching fabric squares.

Comments from the faster learners were,
"I can do this real well!"
"Boy, that was a quick one!"
The slower students could not name all of the shapes. They found the oval difficult.

Large blue charts contained picture stamps with their duplicates on cards for similar matching.

Button Matching. Buttons were glued to a chart and their duplicates were placed on little cards to be matched on the large chart.

Some students divided the cards containing buttons to be matched.

"How many do you have?"

Some children did not always finish the matching.

This was a popular activity, but the faster learners preferred it more (Fig. 10).

Figure 10.   Button matching device.

Tile Matching Chart. A chart was prepared with cardboard discs and a tile on each. An outlined circle was beside each disc into which the matching one was to be placed.

Comments:

"I see where every one goes!"

"Let's do four at a time."

"We did it fast!"

"How do we do this? Oh, I know, like this."

They took turns. Others watched and helped. Some chose to do it again.

Some of the children who usually engaged in solitary play preferred this activity; apparently because it was one that they could easily do alone (Fig. 11).

Figure 11.   Tile matching chart

Fitting Forms to Outlined Shapes. A box of cardboard dics with each containing the outlined shape of a ceramic tile was given to the children. There was a variety of shapes represented in the box. The children were directed to place each tile in its outlined shape on the disc. The shapes were outlined by a felt pen.

This activity was challenging to the faster learners.

Some children laid all of the discs and tiles out on the table before starting. Others took one disc out of the box at a time and matched the tile to it.

They preferred chart activities to the type that involved a variety of items to be placed on the table or desk (Fig. 12).

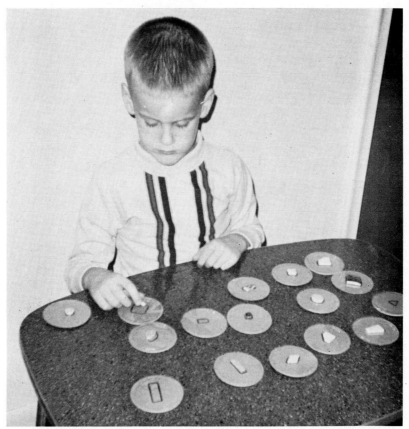

Figure 12.   Matching tile forms and shapes.

Marble Sorting

A chart contained several small aluminum pie plates. A marble was glued by each plate. The children were given marbles and were directed to place the matching ones in each plate. The marbles differed in design and color.

The children enjoyed the make-up of the chart and handling the marbles.

It was considered to be better if the marbles were in solid colors that were more easily distinguished. Some were too similar, and their finer differences were difficult to determine for classification.

This would be a good activity for color recognition, too. It is an independent activity as well as one that can be shared.

A matching chart which involved various groupings of stars was found to be a very versatile favorite with the kindergarten teacher.

Some star groupings were gold, blue, red, etc. Some had a white background; others black. The chart was divided into small squares so that each grouping was distinct and easily determined. Matching cards were similar in groupings, color of stars and background.

The children matched the number of stars involved first, then noticed the correspondence of the color of the card and stars.

This activity required concentration.

They did not count each star in a group at first, but regarded them as sets and matched them for size of group.

When some students went too fast at first and made mistakes they then counted the stars.

The interest was not so great when they first started to use the chart, but it increased and many wanted to do this matching activity.

"I want to do it again."

This chart was meaningful for a variety of reasons:

1. It could be used for number readiness.
2. Color matching was possible.
3. Both groups and individual students could use it.
4. It was a quiet activity that required concentration, but children could work together and help each other, too.
5. It could be used as an independent activity without the teacher's help, but could be also used for instructional purposes (Fig. 13).

Readiness Areas: Language Development, Vocabulary Growth, and Eye-hand Co-ordination.

Device—Picture Vocabulary; Matching Game. A series of cards containing pictures were prepared. The pictures were simple in outline and were not colored. A comprehensive set of small cards each containing one picture was prepared for the teacher to use in

Figure 13.   Matching groupings of colored stars.

"calling" for the game. As each picture was named and held up, the children were to check to see if their cards contained it. If so, they placed a small black construction paper square on the picture. Golf tees may also be used (Fig. 14).

The game was found to be more successful with a group of approximately eleven children. They sat in a semicircle on the floor.

1. The children looked at each other's picture cards before the words were called and indicated matching ones to each other. They also counted their black squares of construction paper.
   Comment:
   "Some guys got seven or eight and I have only five."
2. While the teacher was "calling" the words, if a child didn't

Figure 14. Picture matching game.

have a picture on his card, he would look around to see if others had it and would call the attention of the other students to the fact that their cards contained the picture.

3. Sometimes the children would look at the picture on the small card as it was held up by the teacher and say the name of the picture before she did.

4. Small groups of children would choose the activity during their free period. Others would join them later and ask to play. They would say, "We have started already, but you can play." Then they told the new players what pictures had been called and helped them to get started.

This was extremely popular with the faster students. Some of the same students always rushed to the table to start this game during every activity period.

It was found to be more appealing to the slower students if they were grouped so that they did not have to compete with the faster pupils. This was done after it was found to be discouraging when they could not find the pictures quickly enough to contend with competition.

5. Some children later preferred to play using two or three picture cards at a time.
6. This is beneficial as an independent as well as a supervised activity.

Much conversation, comparing, matching and counting were spontaneously carried on by the children.

Readiness Areas—Critical observation and comparison.

Device—Car Group Matching Chart. Miniature plastic cars of various models and colors were placed in several number groupings on a chart of bristol board.

Corresponding groupings were placed on individual small cards. The children were told to match the cars. The colors and the number of cars in each group matched the same as those on the small cards, but the car models varied.

It was hoped that the children would observe this difference, and they did! Comments were numerous! They greatly enjoyed the chart and made such remarks as, "Oh, boy! She brings us the nicest things to do!"

When they began to do the matching activity, they commented upon the difference in car models. Under the direction of the kindergarten teacher, they described the likenesses and differences involved in the car placement.

More such critical thinking and making of observations should be introduced through some of the pre-reading activities. This instruction should not be first introduced at the time when the child has word-attack skills, word recognition and other areas of formal reading to cope with. Observation, making comparisons and seeing likenesses and differences should start in the pre-reading stage, and then be reinforced through use of a variety of interesting materials to enable the children to have ample time for mastery of these skills before others are introduced. Although readiness begins long before the child is introduced to reading, it continues throughout his lifetime.

GENERAL OBSERVATIONS

1. The charts were preferred most by the children and liked better than other types of activities.

2. Directional awareness was an incidental learning facilitated by the chart activities. When a matching object was placed on the chart, directional differences became apparent.

3. The children who usually engaged in solitary play, seemed to choose independent activities that they could do alone. The activities provided for both group and independent work. We wondered if these children should be encouraged to do activities more with others. It seemed that there was a lack of self-confidence that caused them to choose to work alone rather than interact with others. Perhaps too much working independently can signify lack of self-confidence even though the student can seemingly be self-reliant.

4. Faster students who had been able to do all of the tasks seemed to want more and harder activities. It seemed to suggest a need for more challenge in the planning for the faster students as well as provision for the skills that the slower students lacked.

Austin's *The First R: The Harvard Report on Reading in Elementary School* contains the recommendation that all school systems establish kindergartens; that appropriate reading activities be initiated for those children who are already reading and for those who appear to be ready to begin reading, and that the kindergarten program be adjusted according to each child's strengths and weaknesses as revealed by an appraisal of readiness."[25]

The purpose of this chapter is not to establish kindergarten curriculum goals, but to stress the importance of a more thorough ap-

----

[25]From Mary C. Austin and Coleman Morrison: *The First R: The Harvard Report on Reading in Elementary Schools.* 1963, p. 219. Courtesy of The Macmillan Company, New York.

praisal of the student's readiness abilities during the kindergarten year. Skills in which he lacks ability may be noted. Special provision may help the student who is not ready to read. When a student is retained in kindergarten, it should be a purposeful retention through which instruction is aimed to meet the individual need.

Students who lack any of the readiness skills when they enter first grade should have the benefit of a purposeful program that is planned to provide needed instruction, sufficient repetition, and time for this growth.

An adequate appraisal of the student's readiness status and recommendations by the kindergarten teacher would be very valuable to the teacher of first grade.

5. The provision of these activities and the opportunities for free choice during the activity period were a stabilizing influence upon the kindergartners who usually had difficulty making use of their free time. They began to set goals for themselves and to plan for what they would do. One child said, "When I get this done, I'll do Chart two."

6. Children who had previously needed to ask numerous questions and have much reassurance before they could start an activity began to try to figure out what the directions would probably be. "Oh, I know. This is what you do," etc.

7. The teacher of the kindergarten class observed a growth in pupil respect for property and concern for careful handling of these teacher-prepared instructional materials that was not present as they had previously played with other general toys.

There seem to be several other possibilities for needed exploration in the areas of reading readiness. Some of these needs are as follows.

1. A definite sequential-step listing of the readiness areas and the detailed skills involved.

2. A check-list for teachers of kindergarten and first grade students for use in appraising the readiness status of the children.

3. More evaluation of readiness instructional aids and techniques.

4. Further exploration of other research projects and ways in which school systems have endeavored to help the students who are delayed in readiness skills.

5. Research to determine ways to meet the individual needs of both faster learners who are ready for more challenging activities in the kindergarten as well as those who need a rich and prolonged readiness program before being introduced to formal reading in the first grade.

Chapter VIII

ACTIVITIES FOR SKILL DEVELOPMENT OF RETARDED CHILDREN

W HEN TRAINABLE retarded children come to school, a two-way street for communication is opened to them. Previous to their school entry, there existed the need for them to communicate mainly with their family members only. For some children, their wants were usually quickly forthcoming resulting from a gesture or a nod on their part, and little verbal ability was used or developed.

Another avenue of communication is used when the child wishes to communicate with the family to tell about his school experiences or carry reports from home to school. The motivation for language usage increases through the broader field of interesting things provided for the child to talk about.

Previous to the school experience, many children may not have been motivated to use verbal language any more than necessary to express one or two basic needs. Helping the child to become motivated to communicate with others is one of the important basic instructional goals of the trainable child's curriculum. According to Bernice Baumgartner,

> . . . inability to express himself and be understood by others constitutes perhaps the strongest inhibiting force in the life of the trainable mentally retarded child. Consequently, communicating with others becomes the prime objectives in both home and school. Since the child's behavior pattern seems to be divided between bodily movement and efforts to communicate, the problem for parent and teacher is to transmute the physical movement into communication.
>
> This communication is the core of the educational program for the trainable mentally retarded child, for it is the key that unlocks the door to social adjustment. The child is considered

93

adjusted socially when he can: get along well with other people; understand himself; practice good work habits; follow directions; be well groomed; be trusted; attain personal adequacy in self-care; follow the rules of personal health and safety. But before a child can achieve these goals, he must be able to communicate. [26]

The sequential development of a child's communication provided through action research over a period of years was listed by Bernice Baumgartner. She offered this listing of the learning stages as a guide to help the teacher to know at what level the child is functioning, but she gave the reminder that the child will not necessarily pass through every stage in the sequence. These stages are as follows:

1. The child uses gestures and physical action, but not words to get what he wants.
2. The child tries to use sounds to convey meaning.
3. The child imitates sounds, words and actions: imitating the teacher during an activity; imitating high and low sounds in music; but no words; imitating sounds of others; repeating words on request but not in real situations.
4. The child attempts to verbalize meaningfully; using single

words to include proper names, common exclamations and greetings; identifying objects and pictures with one word; using single words in communicative situations; combining two or more words.

5. The child participates in a group.
6. The child converses with others.[27]

Language is so important in the trainable child's life that it is necessary to begin with building his vocabulary and helping him to learn to communicate with others and follow verbal directions. These skills are also basic for use in activities to promote growth in other learning areas.

---

[26]From Bernice B. Baumgartner: *Helping The Trainable Mentally Retarded Child.* 1960, pp. 3-4. Courtesy of Bureau of Publications Teachers' College Columbia University, New York.

[27]Bernice B. Baumgartner, Ibid. pp. 6-7.

These children can often understand much more than they are able to communicate. They learn to understand spoken words before they can give verbal expression. Helping them to develop both of these types of abilities is needed: *understanding* and *communication*. Activities that build vocabulary and require simple action or following of directions are helpful to begin with in vocabulary development.

Learning Names of Objects. A vocabulary of things in the child's environment can be provided by use of colorful pictures, charts, books or miniature toys or objects.

Actual experiences with real things are most meaningful, but much can be done with pictures, too. Tag board or poster sheets of cardboard may be marked off in squares with a felt pen. A picture may be pasted in each square and the chart thus filled with pictures. The child may name the things on the chart, repeating after the teacher those with which he needs help. Learning to focus his eyes on one object when several others surround it is a beginning step which the child must take in learning to not be distracted as he tries to concentrate. After he is able to find things on the chart, he can look for and name those on a page of a picture book, then proceed to naming things in rows or groups on the page. The child should have much encouragement both at home and in school to learn the names of things in his environment, such as those in the room, what he sees when taking a walk, or other trips with the family, etc. Parents should be encouraged to answer the child's questions, ask questions of him, and to converse with him as much as possible. Verbal language should be expected as the child develops this ability, and he must be provided with many opportunities to express himself verbally (Fig. 15).

The *opaque projector* is very helpful in sustaining pupil interest and increasing the attention span of the trainable child. Books may be used which contain pictures of fruit, vegetables, animals or other categorical groups. As the pages are projected the children may name the items or point to indicate those named by the teacher or other children.

Learning To Follow Verbal Directions. The child may be asked to find certain objects on the chart and point to them. This activity may be done with the class group, or each child may have the

Figure 15. Naming and finding pictured objects.

opportunity to work individually with the teacher to complete
seatwork activities which necessitate following verbal directions. He
may be asked to point to, otherwise indicate, or color certain
objects on a page. The child may also be directed to bring certain things to the teacher or parent, such as table-setting materials,
books, toys, or other objects needed for work and play activities
shared by the child and an adult. A useful chart series for this
vocabulary building activity is the one prepared for kindergarten
children by the Ideal School Supply Co. These contain pictures to
illustrate the consonant sounds, but they may also be used with
the trainable child for learning to name or find certain pictured
objects. Filmstrips may also be used in this way.

Learning Meanings of Some Abstract Words

The trainable child can learn to associate some abstract words with their pictured meanings. Large cards or sheets of construction paper containing three pictures, such as a ball, piano and a girl may be shown to the children. A "key" word may be at the top, such as "music," to be pronounced by the teacher. The child is asked to indicate the picture suggested or represented by the "key" word.

Another card may contain three pictures, such as a cat, pear and a postman. A "key" picture, such as that of a milkman may be at the top. The teacher may say, "The milkman helps us by bringing milk to our homes. Find someone else who helps us."

Other cards may contain several pictures. The child may be asked to find a picture of something to use when we eat, play, etc. Other variations which require the association of words with meanings may be used (Fig. 16).

The Children May Learn To Relate Common Objects with Things That Are Associated with Them

A chart may contain pictures of various things (a lamp, envelope, etc.). The teacher may have a box of real objects that are associated with the pictured objects, such as a light bulb, letter and other things. A child is asked to find the related picture for each object as it is held up in view. Each picture and object may be named as the indication is made. Sentences may be used to describe or answer questions about the objects. The children may also play a game in which they take turns choosing someone to match objects with their related pictures as they are held up. They may describe or dramatize experiences suggested by the objects. A child may dramatize how the postman puts a letter in the box, and the teacher describes his actions as they are presented. (Yes, he opens the box, he puts the letter in, he closes the box," etc.) (Fig. 17).

A large picture of a table setting may be shown. A real fork, knife, etc. may be available so that a complete setting can be prepared. The teacher may hold up each place-setting item and ask a child to indicate each one on the chart and note its location. The children may make up sentences or repeat some said by the

Figure 16. Indicating related pictures.

teacher. "I hold my spoon in my hand." "My napkin goes on my lap," etc. "Right" and "left," "this side" and "that side" could be used in sentences as the children take turns setting the table scene. They may practice placing the table-setting items in their proper places. A large chart containing real items in their proper places for a table setting could be displayed in the room.

Activities To Promote Growth in Coordination

Before the children are ready for activities requiring skill in finer eye-hand coordination, they need to learn gross bodily control. Sequential skill development which will prepare the child to later learn to print his name or master tasks requiring finer eye-hand

Figure 17. Matching objects with related pictures.

coordination can be accomplished in gym activities and in the classroom.

Eye-body Coordination (Gross bodily control in eye and body coordination skills)

Learning To Skip: Before effort is made to teach structured and disciplined bodily control, the child must first have had preliminary experiences, such as free play in the gym and on the playground, running, bouncing and throwing a ball, and many other spontaneous self-directed skill building opportunities.

Steps in Learning To Skip

1. The teacher stands by the child and helps him to alternately

lift the right and left foot and put each foot down, saying, "Up", "Down."

2. The teacher then helps the child to alternately hop up and down on the right and left foot, saying, "Up", "Down." The child stands in the same place during this phase.

3. The teacher helps the child to move forward, hopping on right and left foot, saying, "Up", "Down."

Learning To Control Body To Follow Patterns on Floor

1. **Walking on Patterns.** The teacher may place small pieces of masking tape in two rows at spaced intervals on the floor leaving sufficient room between the rows to permit the child to walk comfortably.

The teacher then instructs and helps the child to walk down the rows, stepping on a piece of tape at each step.

Some children can learn to skip every other piece of tape or alternate their feet from right to left as they walk (Fig. 18).

2. **Matching Feet to Corresponding Color Pattern.** The teacher may place construction paper circles of two colors, such as red and blue, in a line at random on the floor.

A circle of one color is fastened on the child's right foot and one of the other color on the left. The child is directed to walk across the path of the circles placing the foot containing the circle of one color on a circle of its corresponding color on the floor. His foot may be placed on a floor space between circles as he maintains his balance sufficiently to find a suitable circle on which to step. Anything goes as long as the one basic rule is followed (Fig. 19).

3. **Using Hands and Feet Together.** The teacher may place two paper towels on the floor and direct the child to stand on them. Two towels are placed in front of the child. He is then directed and helped to step on the two front towels and move the back ones to the front. He continues to walk, stepping on two towels and moving two forward. It is easier for some children to learn by using just one towel to stand on and one to move forward at first, then later use two.

The teacher may place construction paper circles on the floor. The child is directed to walk and bounce a ball and try to hit a circle at each bounce. Some children can learn this skill by standing still, bouncing the ball and hitting a circle, catching

Figure 18.   Walking on patterns.

the ball as it comes up, then starting over again. Others will soon be able to run and bounce the ball and hit the circles and keep going.

4. Exercise for the Whole Body

Gerald Wargo suggested a series of "Pretend Games" that need no equipment, yet exercise the entire body. They are in sequence.

Pretend Game Number One Is Called Statues. "We are beautiful marble statues. We stand very straight and tall. Because we are made of stone, we cannot move even a finger or an eyelash. Suddenly and very slowly we come to life. We blink our eyes, move our heads carefully, around and around, hunch our

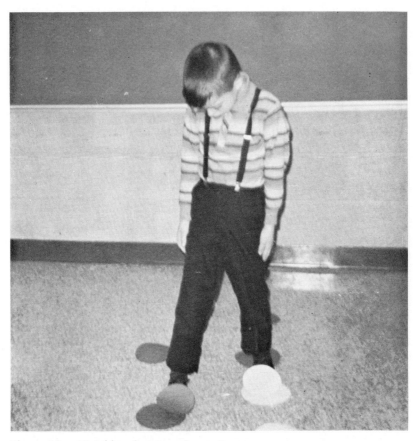

Figure 19.   Matching feet to color patterns.

shoulders up and down a few times, move our fingers one by one, bend our knees, lift up our right feet and then our left feet, shake both hands, hunch our shoulders up and down many times and twist our heads from right to left."

This game loosens up the muscles in the body.

Other pretend games in sequence exercise the muscles in the arms and shoulders, the trunk, neck and head, build the legs and the back and provide a source of exercise for the feet and legs.[28]

---

[28]From Gerald J. Wargo, Physical education and recreation of mentally retarded children. *The Physical Educator,* May, 1961, pp. 65-6, Vol. 18, No. 2. Courtesy of Phi Epsilon Kappa Fraternity.

The child benefits from activities to develop large-muscle skills. Gerald J. Wargo stated that motion is that which produces muscle strength and flexibility in all children. He warns that it should not be wasted motion, but needs to be channeled to the development of timing and co-ordination: in other words, it should be *profitable motion*. He presented several different outlets through which profitable motion can be accomplished. They include games, exercises, swimming, walking, etc.[29]

Gross Eye-hand Coordination Skill

1. **Finding Specified Large Objects:** The teacher may name certain toys and direct the children to bring them from the toy box.

The children may be directed to bring specified things from the shelf or other places in the room.

2. **Making Pegboard Designs:** The teacher may make designs and ask the children to copy them. They may take turns preparing designs and calling on each other to duplicate them.

3. **Felt Designs:** They may be made with felt scraps on the felt board.

4. **Torn Paper designs** from construction paper are helpful in development of coordination skills as well as providing means of artistic expression.

5. **Sponge designs** may be made by dipping squares of sponge in paint and placing them on paper. One or several colors of paint may be used.

6. **Water color designs** are a favorite with the children. After they have had ample opportunity to "paint anything they want to," they will reach the skill level where they can purposely paint trees, cars, houses, and other familiar things.

7. *Finger paint* serves different needs with different children. Some who have been taught to keep themselves neat and clean at first have misgivings about putting their hands into a "mess". Encouragement and help in making preparation, which may include putting newspapers on their desks, wearing protective paint aprons or shirts, and washing their hands when finished, will possibly motivate them to realize that there are acceptable times when playing in something "gooey" can be fun. Others will soon be able to really "go creative" as they

---

[29]Gerald J. Wargo, *Ibid.* p. 65.

derive great enjoyment from experimenting with this medium of expression. The earlier the children can profitably start with finger paint the better. Parents should be encouraged to let them finger paint at home, especially five or six year olds who may not have been able to enter school yet (Fig. 20).

Figure 20.   Fun with finger paint.

Activities for Finer Eye-hand Coordination

1. **Learning To Color** (a) Squares, circles or triangles may be cut from bristol or poster board, thus making a stencil.

The teacher may help the child to trace around the opening within the stencil, then look at the outlined figure before fitting the stencil back over the outline and coloring within the space. The child should be helped to keep the stencil over the outline as he colors, and this insures success as he begins the first step of coloring. This will also give the child the "feel" of the boundary within which he is to color. Stencils, simple in pattern, from the dime store may also be used. (b) Embroidery hoops may be wrapped securely with masking tape and used by the child to place on the paper and color within the frame. Help must be given by the teacher to enable the child to hold the ring in place as he colors. This activity helps him to become aware of the surface within which he is to color.

A safety game may be played as the child colors. The teacher and child may pretend that the circles are lights. The teacher may say "Color the green light. What does it mean?" The child may answer the questions. "I am coloring the light that says go," etc.

Some children will be able to trace around other boxes, lids, or other objects of various shapes, and color within the areas.

(c) Square, round or triangular outlines may be made by pasting strips of construction paper on white paper, thus making an area within which it will be easy for the child to color. This will enable the child to be aware of the area within and to distinguish it from the surrounding ground. This is a very successful device for teaching very young trainable children to color (Fig. 21).

(d) The next steps are to learn to color within areas having wide lines drawn by crayon or felt pen, then finer lines. Pictures with more complicated details can be attempted after the child has learned to stay within easy surfaces and to distinguish figures, ground, and parts of pictures as related to wholes.

2. **Learning To Use Scissors:** The child should have ample opportunity to experiment with blunt scissors before any formal effort is made to teach their use. Parents of pre-school trainable children should be encouraged to let the child use scissors at home under supervision. What may seem to be aimless snipping of paper into pieces is important learning for the child as he becomes skillful in manipulating the scissors. Parents may be instructed to help the child at home in the same way that help is given at school. Much individual help is needed for the retarded child who is attempting to learn to use scissors. This is one reason why it is so important for teachers and parents to

Figure 21.   Device for learning to color.

not only work together but also to share the same instructional
aims and techniques.

Plastic safety scissors that parents need not be concerned
with danger in permitting their child to use them freely and
independently are available at many stores or toy departments
and are inexpensive. A firm that offers them is listed in the
Appendix.

Construction-paper strips may be pasted at spaced intervals
on white paper, on which the child will make his first attempt
to do directed or structured cutting. The teacher will then show
the child how to place the thumb and first finger through the
handle rings. With the teacher holding the top of the thumb
handle slightly, the child can then learn to open and close the

scissors. The words "open" and "close" can be used as instruction is given. The child may practice opening and closing the
scissors before any attempt is made to cut.

Next, help is given as the child attempts to cut on the wide
construction paper lines. Success is insured at the first attempt
with individual help. Much practice and help with cutting on
the construction paper lines will enable the child to realize
that cutting involves staying on a line. The children enjoy this
effort with individual help and will frequently ask to use
scissors. They still should have opportunities to use the scissors
independently at their seats (Fig. 22).

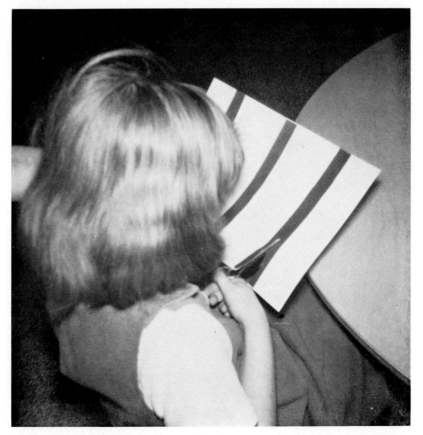

Figure 22.   Learning to cut on wide lines.

The next step involves learning to stay on other wide lines

drawn by a felt pen or crayon. Finer lines are introduced as the child becomes ready. Some children will be able to do much more intricate cutting. Magazines for pictures, Christmas cards, and catalogs should be readily available to the children for cutting out anything they wish whenever they choose during free time as well as for directed use of scissors.

3. **Learning To Trace:** The tracing of wide lined figures comes next, then tracing broken lines. More complicated figures to trace should be introduced as the child is ready for them. The individual differences in children's abilities and chronological age play a part in when tracing skills are developed (Fig. 23).

Figure 23.   Tracing on wide lines.

Tracing of one's own name or names of other children will provide purposeful practice.

Activities to Promote Gross Visual Discrimination Skills

1. Learning To Do Simple Matching

(a) **Puzzles** can be prepared involving very simple shapes, such as circles, squares and triangles, drawn with a felt pen. A shape is contained in each boxed section of the puzzle. Sets of cards with shapes corresponding to those on the puzzles are given to the child to match each one by placing it in its proper place. The puzzles can be used over and over individually by the children as independent activities after learning to match the shapes (Fig. 24).

Figure 24. Puzzle for gross visual skill in matching.

(b) **Fabric matching puzzles** can be made from scraps obtained from upholstery or wallpaper sample books. Corresponding sets of cards containing the same fabric samples can be given to the children to place each card on its proper place on the puzzle (Fig. 25).

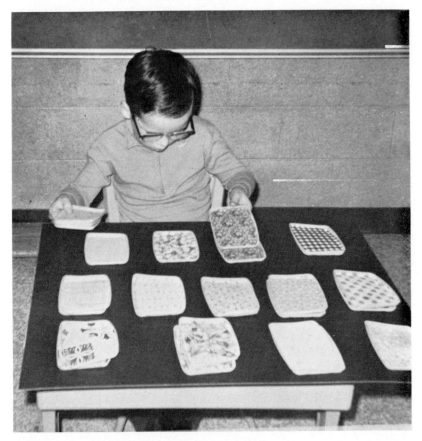

Figure 25.   Fabric matching puzzle.

(c) **A fabric matching game** can be played by the children for fun and also to strengthen their ability to discriminate likenesses.

A set of cards involving various fabrics may be prepared. A set of numerous fabric cards which are small and contain only one fabric are used by the teacher to hold up one at a time in view of the children and say, "Do you have a red one like this?" The children who may have the indicated fabric patterns may place golf tees or other small objects on the corresponding ones on their cards. The child whose card is filled first wins. The children may take turns being in charge of holding up the cards. This game involves language ability as well as visual discrimination and eye-hand coordination.

(d) **Egg Carton Device:** This is to help the child to learn to match pictures or colors.

A small circle or square of colored construction paper is placed in each compartment of an egg carton. A set of small cards of various colors are given to the child to match the colors by placing each small card in the compartment containing its corresponding color.

Gummed pictures of flowers, animals, birds, etc., which are available at stationery or five and ten-cent stores may be placed in the egg carton device and corresponding sets for each may may be prepared for the children to match.

The children may make egg carton devices as an independent seatwork activity and later take them home to match their contents as a leisure time activity.

(e) **Charts** or poster board sheets may contain colors, pictures or shapes, one in each square compartment. The children may be shown various cards containing pictures, colors, or shapes, and they may take turns finding similar ones on the chart. (Fig. 26)

Development of Finer Visual Discrimination

1. Matching Related Things

(a) Charts or large sheets of paper may be divided into two sides by a wide line or black ribbon down the middle. Headings, such as "Clothes for Boys" and "Clothes for Girls," "Things for Work" and "Things for Play," etc., may be printed at the top of each side. Pictures related to these topics may be held up by the teacher, and the children may indicate their proper side on the chart. They may be pinned to the chart, then taken down and the activity repeated over and over (Fig. 27).

Clothing, tools, toys and many things may be matched.

(b) A chart may have pictures of mother animals down one side, a line through the middle, and pictures of baby animals down the other side. A string that is attached to each mother animal may contain a golf tee, large button or other object at the end which the child may use to point to the corresponding baby animal (Fig. 28).

Figure 26. Chart for matching shapes.

(c) A chart may contain large objects on one side and corresponding small ones on the other side. The child may match them.

2. *Matching Letters*

(a) **Cards or Charts.** A chart may be marked into large squares with a wide marking pen and a letter printed in each square. A corresponding set of cards may be made to contain the same letters. As each card is indicated, a child may find its corresponding letter on the chart.

(b) **Egg Carton Devices.** Letters may be placed in the individual compartments of egg cartons. Milk bottle tops or other small circles may each contain a letter. The child may

Figure 27. Classifying related things.

place each small circle with its letter in the compartment that contains a matching letter.

3. Matching Words

Charts or large sheets of poster board may contain the names of the children in the class, safety or self care words. Sets of small cards which include the same words for each chart may be made for the children to match to the large charts. As the teacher holds up each small card, the children may find and indicate its matching word. The charts may also be placed on a child's desk, and may be matched by individual students or small groups who work together (Fig. 29).

Seatwork sheets may involve matching of letters, words or

Figure 28.   Matching mother and baby animals.

names. Some children will be able to paste words in their proper places on a sheet of paper, and others who have mastered the use of scissors and have a longer attention and interest span will be able to cut boxed words out and complete the pasting independently.

This type of seatwork may also be prepared on cards for more permanent use. The seatwork lessons may be used again and again at various times, and as the children "outgrow" them, the cards may be kept for use later with other children as they become ready for this learning. The matching cards, etc. may be kept in envelopes and stapled to the charts for storage.

4. Vision Screening Skills

Most trainable retarded children may have their vision screened by a technician when this service is available through the health department to the public school where the class may be housed.

A prerequisite to the child's ability to profit from vision testing is a readiness program consisting of eye-hand coordination skills, following directions and growth in visual perception skills, including some of the previously described techniques.

The children can learn through special training to follow the directions and give the responses required by the Massachusetts Vision Test. This testing is followed by the referral of the child to an ophthalmologist if the test result indicates the need for medical aid.

The children need preparatory training in developmental sequence in preparation for being tested by the technician and to

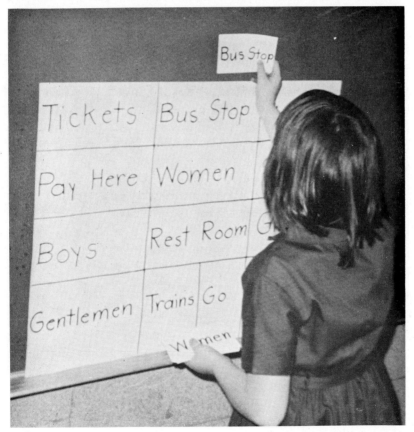

Figure 29. Matching functional words.

respond to the mechanical Massachusetts vision testing devices through valid indications.

1. Although some children may be able to follow directions, they need special preparation to enable them not to be distracted by the mechanical device.

2. They need to be able to look into the device and simultaneously use their hands or fingers to indicate the directions of the letters in the test.

3. They must learn to not be confused by various sizes of letters.

4. Some children will need special help because they may be unable to verbally indicate the positions of a ball in relation to a box in one test item.

5. They need training in visual perception and eye-hand coordination skills to enable them to communicate what they can or cannot see.

Activities and their accompanying techniques and materials to develop the children's abilities to see likenesses and differences have been described in the Gross Visual Discrimination section of this chapter. This was followed by those activities involving finer discrimination of likenesses and differences in shapes, letters, and words through use of various visual aids, such as charts, flannel board, chalk board and seatwork activities.

When the children are able to understand directions, to look for specified things, can communicate what they see, and have sufficient interest and attention span, they are ready for instruction directly applicable to the Vision Test.

In preparation for the vision screening, the following instructional aids may be used with the children in the classroom:

A large black letter E is printed on a card. When the card is held up, down, left or right, the children are directed individually to indicate the direction of the letter by pointing with their fingers.

Some children will need kinesthetic experience to "feel" the direction of the letter before they can visualize it.

The teacher and child may work together as the child's finger is guided to "trace" the lines in the letter's direction. Verbal indication of the letter should be given each time. "It is pointing this way."

A movable letter E may be fastened to a card, with a paper fastener, thus giving much opportunity for practice.

Cards with smaller letters may be used next (Fig. 30).

Figure 30.   Learning to indicate letter directions.

An oblong white construction paper frame may be placed on a black background. A little red construction paper circle, called a "ball" is placed in various positions in relation to the frame "box." The children are directed to indicate the position of the ball, such as "In the box," "On the line" "Out of the box." A similar ball and box card may be placed on the child's desk. As the teacher places the ball in a position on a card, the child is asked to copy its position by placing the ball where he sees it on his card (Fig. 31).

Figure 31. Indicating the position in which the ball is seen.

Cards should next be made to resemble those which the children will be exposed to on the vision test. The cards contain a large letter C on an orange background and a letter D on a green background. Two rows of E's in various positions follow on a white background. Practice with these cards helps the children to not be distracted by several letters in a row. The teacher points to the letters one at a time, and the children respond by indicating their direction.

An instructional device may be made from a cardboard box and used to help the children learn to look into the vision testing device and indicate their reactions to the letter positions by pointing. The top of the box may have an open strip in back to enable the teacher to insert cards containing letter positions and hold them at the back of the box. Two other small square openings are in the top of the box at the front. A white paper strip is fastened across the front of the box. The child rests his head against this as he looks into the "machine." A square view-opening is in front below the white strip. The children take turns sitting at a desk, looking into the box and pointing to indicate the positions of the letters as the teacher points to each with a pencil (Fig. 32).

Figure 32. Learning to use the vision screening "machine."

One item on the test requires the children to look through a pair of "magic glasses." A pair of "magic glasses" should be made from cardboard for use in preparation for that item on the test.

The "magic glasses" should fit into the two openings in the top of the "machine." The children must learn to indicate by a "Yes" or "No" answer when asked if they can see through the magic glasses. A piece of dark paper may be placed over the "lenses" to prevent them from being able to see through them sometimes during the practice lessons. Sufficient practice should be given to enable the children to really be able to indicate whether or not they can see through the glasses to facilitate the presentation of this item in the vision test.

Supplementary independent activities which require the children to follow similar directions on paper should follow the instruction and group activities.

Worksheets may involve rows of E's on which the children are directed to mark or point to the others in each row that are in the same position as the first one for each row.

Other sheets may contain an outlined "box and a ball" in some position in relation to the box. The other half of the sheet may just have the outlined "box." The children may be instructed to draw the ball as it is pictured on the other half of the sheet.

Individual learning abilities of the students as well as their handicaps, such as visual perceptual disabilities and difficulties concerning directionality, will cause their performance in the vision testing skills to be influenced in some of the following ways:

1. Some children will need a much longer period to master these skills. They may not be able to be screened the first year that they are introduced to this instruction.

2. Most children need a review practice and the opportunity to use the instructional materials before each screening session. The children's vision is rescreened once during each school year in most schools.

3. There may be some severely handicapped children who cannot learn to have their vision screened in this way. The Health Department has now available a simpler testing device for children who cannot follow the directions of the Massachusetts Vision Screening Test. This easier device involves responses to how the children see in relation to a cloud, bunny, grass, etc. They are asked to give verbal responses involving these items.

This device is often used with preschool and kindergarten children.

After the use of the instructional materials and mastery of the skills involved, some children will be ready to have their vision screened (Fig. 33).

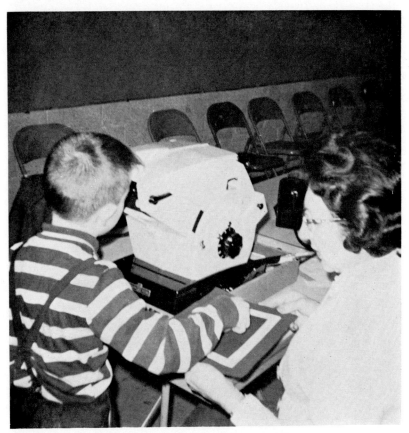

Figure 33.   The child is ready for the vision screening.

A visit to the ophthalmologist is recommended for the children who are referred for this additional vision evaluation and correction. Parents of those who cannot perform on the school screening items should also be advised to consult an ophthalmologist for his evaluation and correctional recommendations if any are considered necessary.

Science for the Trainable Child

The trainable child differs from others in learning ability, but he has the same needs as other children. He has a curiosity to know about the world in which he lives, is interested in animals, and loves to see and learn about new things. This child is in a special class because he has a unique learning handicap and a need for us to provide for his differences, but the mere fact that he is a child demands our consideration for his likenesses to other children.

A science curriculum involves experiences in the child's immediate environment no matter how limited may be his scope. Science offers many opportunities for easy motivation of the child's desire to learn and also readily appeals to his interest. An exciting new challenge exists whenever he sees a toad in the garden, a butterfly in his yard or a cloud threatening to bring a weather change. The world of science is at the child's doorstep and is an avenue leading him to exciting new adventure.

Although his learning abilities are limited, the trainable child can know the joy of seeing and petting baby farm-animals or handling a starfish and listening to the ocean echoed in a shell. The extent to which these children will travel to see the interesting sights in their land is possibly not very great, but through teaching science we can bring many faraway experiences to them and cause their immediate environment to be more meaningful. Evidences of their interest and appreciation may be apparent through attentive listening, enthusiastic participation and sharing their learning experiences at home.

Interesting science activities stimulate the child's desire to communicate with others and grow in language skills. The children love to share school experiences with their parents, and when the learning is very interesting, there will be important things to talk about. Motivating the child to verbally communicate is very necessary for speech and language growth. Speech and self-expression are utilized through science learnings and activities, such as observing the moon and stars at home, in which both child and parent participate together.

Sensory training, ability to see likenesses and differences and to make simple classifications, are necessary aims that are possible through skill-building activities for the trainable child. Such an abundance of various means through which these goals can be achieved exists in the realm of science.

There are so many helpful audiovisual aids to make science real to the child. The opaque and overhead projector, films and filmstrips, and so many others meet the need many times and aid the growth of attention and interest span. The trainable child can help to operate some of the equipment, and such a privilege is greatly appreciated.

There are many ways for science to be correlated with other aspects of the curriculum. Finger plays, poems, handicraft activities, music, speech skill, can all be related to science learning. Short units in which there are many activities as well as interesting information presented by the teacher in a variety of ways to hold the child's interest should be included in the science curriculum.

Science offers valuable contributions to the general child development goals which are important for trainable children. Outcomes in the following are a result of science experiences.

Mental Health

1. The child can feel more secure and adequate through his ability to contribute to group activities.
    a. By bringing science specimens to school.
    b. By participating in class activities and experiments.
2. The child can experience success through easy but interesting activities.
    a. By learning names of new things.
    b. By being able to verbalize and communicate more.

Attitudes and Habits

1. The child's interest in the world in which he lives can be increased and he can gain more appreciation of the things he has to enjoy.
    a. Through his realization of the beauty of insects, birds, flowers, and others.
    b. Through more awareness of nature around his home and school.
2. The child grows in ability to share, play and work with others.
3. He can know the joy of learning.

4. He has the opportunity to respect and be kind to animals as he learns about them.

5. The child realizes that his contribution to the group activities is important.

6. He also realizes the importance of the contributions of other children.

Language Development

1. The child's speaking vocabulary can be increased.

   a. Through learning science meanings.

   b. Through learning names of insects, parts of plants, names of birds, etc.

2. The child can learn more verbal expression.

   a. Through reporting the results of experiments or activities.

   b. By sharing experiences.

   c. By reporting home experiences related to school activites.

   d. By playing science games.

   e. By telling about pictures and answering questions.

   f. By asking questions.

   g. By classifying and naming things related to the science study.

3. The children can learn to listen and understand others.

Visual Abilities: Discrimination and Memory

1. The child's ability to see likenesses and differences grows through the following.

   a. Through learning how things are different and how they are alike.

   b. Through learning names and making groupings of things alike.

2. The child learns how to see differences in sizes.

3. The child learns to become more aware of changes.

Social Participation and Adjustment

1. The child learns to become more independent and responsible.

2. He learns to use equipment safely and take care of it.

3. He learns to make use of materials available to him.

4. The child learns to share responsibility and materials.

5. The child learns to participate with others yet be responsible individually, too.

The science curriculum should include things that are in the child's daily life, because *the purpose of science for the trainable child is to help him to become more aware of and gain more pleasure from his environment.*

Learning how to care for pets leads to lessons about farm and zoo animals. Learning basic things about plants makes taking care of one's garden more interesting. Learning names of fruits and vegetables and how to classify them cause the children to realize why it is important to eat them and how they are beneficial in one's diet. Their daily activities, no matter how sheltered they may be, bring them in contact with many areas to be included in an interesting science curriculum.

There is a great range of individual differences in abilities and interests even in these severely handicapped children. Science offers many opportunities to provide for these differences.

Parents are so eager to help their child in any way possible. Assignments can be given in which both parent and child can work together to enable the child to become more aware of the beauty around him.

When we consider the ways in which all children need enlightenment to realize the world of science to the extent of their abilities, we cannot fail to be aware of possibilities for the trainable children to benefit from such a program filled with beauty and interest.

Emphasis has been placed upon the need for teachers of the trainable retarded to devise materials, techniques and instructional devices that meet the unique need of the child. Commercial and other general materials are very helpful, but nothing can be more important than teacher-prepared devices that have been proven successful by a teacher in achieving certain instructional aims.

The value of teacher-devised instructional aids has been emphasized. Their uniqueness lies in their specific application to the skill being presented and in their provision for sequential development.

Language growth, coordination and visual discrimination are part of the necessary background learning which facilitates success for the child in other efforts whether these be in self-care, communication or useful work tasks.

Curriculum Goals for the Trainable Child

Although the curriculum for any child includes all of his experiences both at home and in school as well as all other life activities, this fact has special significance for the trainable child. There is a greater need for the home and school to supplement the child development goals of each other to cause them to become meaningful in the life of the trainable retarded child.

The scope of the curriculum is the accounting of these experiences in preparation for the child's taking part in society to the extent of his potential. It is difficult to predict just what the severely retarded child will be able to do later, and so it is difficult to appraise the child's experiences. The need exists, however, for instructional goals to be planned and evaluated in accordance with both the long-range and the short-range of the child's growth. The child's present needs must be met as well as plans made for his future.

Parents must consider their means in planning for their child and for his later care and guidance. Through the school efforts, they may become aware of their child's limitations and understand his learning potential. They may be helped through guidance offered to do this needed planning.

The following general objectives of the curriculum have been cited as very important to the child now as well as in preparation for his adult life.

1. *Self-Care*. The child should be helped and encouraged to assume as much responsibility as possible for dressing himself, using habits of cleanliness, etc.
2. *Economic Usefulness*. Helping at home and sharing the housekeeping tasks are important ways for the child to help in his society.
3. *Safety*. Learning to read street signs, crossing the road carefully and playing safely.
4. *Health*. Learning to eat proper foods, using good health habits, etc.

5. *Motor Coordination.* Activities to develop both large and small muscle co-ordination are necessary.

6. *Communication Skills.* Oral language is a most important aspect stressed in the classroom. The child should be encouraged to speak at home as much as possible.

7. *Social Adjustment.* Learning to work and play with others, share toys, take turns, etc., are especially important.

8. *Knowledge of the World About Him.* Learning about community helpers, what to do if he is lost, care of pets, family trips, and wonderful adventures that are so important to the child.

9. *Recreational and Diversional Activities.* Physical education through gym class and playground at school, ball games with children at home, etc.

10. *Aesthetic Appreciation.* Learning to love music, art and stories at school and in the home.

11. *Self-concept.* Learning to understand and accept what they cannot do and working to learn to do their best. Realizing that they are important as persons and that they belong to the group.

12. *Spiritual Development.* Learning to share with and be kind to each other.

13. *Emotional Adjustment.* Learning to adjust to situations in which they cannot have their own way and learning to know what is acceptable behavior.[30]

Functional Reading

Some trainable mentally retarded children may be able to recognize a limited sight vocabulary consisting of emergency words, their names and addresses and the names of their classmates. Some individual children have been able to reach a level of word recognition at the preprimer and primer stage to enable them to derive pleasure from picture and easy story books. Some other individual students have been reported to have reached a higher level of word sight recognition.

The following is a list of some words that the children may

[30]From Harold M. Williams: *Education of The Severely Retarded Child,* OE-35022 Bulletin. 1961, No. 20, pp. 29-30. Courtesy of the U.S. Department of Health, Education and Welfare.

profit from learning to recognize for protection and to meet daily emergencies.

POLICE STATION	OUT	REST ROOM
OUT OF ORDER	IN	LADIES
PAY AS YOU ENTER	GO	GENTLEMEN
TICKET OFFICE	STOP	MEN
USE OTHER DOOR	OFFICE	WOMEN
PULL	PLEASE	SCHOOL
PUSH	PRIVATE	FIRE STATION
WET PAINT	UP	BOYS
PUBLIC TELEPHONE	DOWN	GIRLS
WATCH YOUR STEP	NO ADMITTANCE	
KEEP TO RIGHT	QUIET	

Trips and real experiences involving the use of these words are important for helping the children to become aware of their conceptual meanings as well as the sight recognition. Dramatizations and role playing in which the meanings are presented are also very helpful.

There is the need for flexibility and adaptability of materials for the instruction of the trainable retarded. Readiness workbooks prepared for beginners in the regular classes are inappropriate for their needs as such, but some of their pages may be adapted for individual student help in picture recognition, matching and other individual skills.

Some of the large picture charts used by kindergartners and first graders may be utilized for picture recognition and language skill development for the trainable children if they are carefully adapted to these needs.

Special adaptation of many instructional materials and audio-visual equipment to the instructional goals planned for the trainable retarded children may be done in accordance with teacher creativity and ability to prepare instructional aids designed for unique learning needs, abilities and limitations.*

---

*The activities for language development, learning names of new objects, following verbal directions, abstract word meanings, use of scissors, and matching feet to corresponding colors originally appeared in "Language Development for the Trainable" by Mary Lou Durbin, *The Pointer for Special Class Teachers and Parents of the Handicapped* (Vol. II, No. 2, 1966, pp. 44-47. The Association for Special Class Teachers and Parents of the Handicapped, Inc.).

Chapter IX

PARENT CONTRIBUTIONS TO PRE-SCHOOL
READINESS

R EADING READINESS is present when a child has reached the
maturational level in all skill areas to permit him to learn to read
readily and with pleasure. The child is now ready to profit from
reading instruction because he has mastered all preceding skills
that are basic in his preparation for the reading accomplishment.

The need for a child to not be expected to learn to read until
he is ready is as apparent as the fact that a baby cannot be expected
to begin walking until he has gained the needed coordination skills
that enable him to attempt this new ambulatory task. It is, therefore, very necessary for parents to understand the importance of
their child's readiness for reading and how it is comprised of all
of his life experiences which begin years before he enters school.

This effort to offer some suggested ways in which many parents
of preschoolers can contribute to their child's readiness for reading
has been done for the purpose of sharing ideas relating to the
utilization of materials and opportunities within the child's home.
Most parents sincerely wish to help their children to prepare for a
happy and successful start in school and wish to avoid the "If I
had only known this before he started" regrets.

Whatever the advantages enjoyed by the child in his home environment or the lack of them are, much more can be done by the
parents who are more aware of what the school personnel are
attempting to do for the student and how they, the parents, can
contribute to the success of this endeavor. The aim of this chapter is therefore being directed toward helping parents realize just
how important readiness is, some factors involved in readiness,
and the influence of the home upon a child's preparation for
reading.

This presentation of readiness skills and practical ways in which parents can help during the preschool years that precede the readiness stage involves the use of materials that most parents would have available in their homes or would easily be able to obtain. Instructional devices that can be prepared from scrap or inexpensive materials to teach readiness skills are described.

A description of a summer program involving preschoolers, their parents and prepared instructional materials and techniques contrived and devised from only the media and materials easily available to parents stresses the fact that readiness instruction of an exceptionally high order may be achieved by parents in the home several years before the child starts school and may be continued to supplement the child's school activities after he begins reading. Such parental awareness and involvement may play an important role in the prevention of reading problems, or the solving of them when they exist. The child's preparation for school can thus provide him with the self-confidence so necessary for successful achievement in any new venture.

The Child Helps at Home

Parents can help in preparing their child to assume responsibilities for completing assignments, listening to directions, and to grow sufficiently in independence, work habits and readiness for other school tasks if they encourage and help him to share in the responsibilities at home. The child who rarely hangs up his own coat, puts away toys after play only when constantly reminded to do so, and has nothing to do that he can feel is contributing to the happiness of the home cannot as readily adopt worthwhile work habits at school as the competent child who has enjoyed sharing a do-your-part home life.

"What can I do to help?" parents often ask when they become aware of their child's difficulty with reading. In too many cases, this question is asked seven or eight years too late. Many reading authorities emphasize the need to begin early in preparing the child for reading readiness. Opinions of some authorities are as follows:

Soon after birth the child begins to acquire experience essential for learning to read.[31]

---

[31]*Reading Difficulties: Their Diagnosis and Correction,* by Guy L. Bond and Miles A. Tinker. Copyright © 1957, by Appleton-Century-Crofts, Inc. Reprinted by permission of Appleton-Century-Crofts.

Many environmental factors condition the rate of development up to the time when the child is ready to read. To acquire auditory and visual skills together with language facility, there must be opportunity and guidance. In addition to his meeting a broad range of experiences, the child must be stimulated to discriminate sounds and objects, and to listen to and use words. It is important for older persons to talk to and with the child while he looks at pictures and talks about them. Also, his own extensive experience with such materials as picture books, crayons, paper, scissors, paint brushes, etc. plays a role in his preparation for reading.[32]

Charlotte Mergentime stressed the need for parents to begin early in their child's life to prepare him for readiness.

"You can begin when your child is in the cradle."[33]

Experiences Shared by Parent and Child

The experiences that help reading to be meaningful to a child begin early in his life and are continuous. Such experiences as trips, visits to a farm or dairy, train station or airport as well as many others are important to his readiness for reading. Other real life experiences that involve learning the names of new things, handling, touching, tasting and hearing also help the child to form vivid mental images as he reads the word symbols for these things that he has experienced. As he sees the word "train," he forms a mental image or thought picture of how a train looks, the sound of the whistle, and if he has been to a train station or taken a ride on a train, he may mentally visualize the trees and houses as he passed them or remember the sound of the wheels on the tracks and how this movement felt to him. The word symbol for train will be much more meaningful to him than to the child who may have merely seen trains at a railroad crossing or in pictures.

There is a familiar old story about how several blind men gave their impressions of how an elephant must look after they had each touched a part of the animal's body. One man who had touched the trunk thought that it must resemble a rope. Another who had touched the elephant's side thought surely it must be flat like a wall. Children who must attempt to form mental images of

---

[32]Guy L. Bond and Miles A. Tinker, Ibid. p. 20.
[33]Charlotte Mergentime, *You and Your Child's Reading*. © 1963, p. 34. Courtesy of Harcourt, Brace and World, Inc., New York.

how objects must look when reading about something with which they have had little or no experience are just as limited in their perceptions as the blind men who wished to describe an elephant. The child who has a broad experiential background can form varied and interesting impressions and gain deeper meaning from written descriptions in his reading book.

Parents can do much to help their child to have a wide range of experiences at his disposal as he prepares to learn to read.

Helping the Child To Become Confident

What parents have done to prepare their child for the thrilling new adventure that school can be for him influences his readiness for reading as well as his ability to make new friends and view the world as a happy place in which he is important, confident and competent. Such a feeling about himself will help him to understand that the contributions of others are important, too.

Negative or threatening things that are said to the child about school can do much harm to his attitude about starting.

Background Experiential Influences

The home environment, family life activities and how each member of the family contributes to the child's happiness and self-confidence all are significant to the child's preparation for school and success in reading.

> Above all, the ideal home should give the child a sense of security and a realization that he is a loved and welcome member of the family group. His efforts to do what is expected of him should be encouraged and praised so that he may develop confidence in himself.[34]
>
> In families broken by separation or divorce, every effort should be made to allow the child to experience some companionship with each parent so he does not feel that he is totally missing what other children with both parents are experiencing.[35]

Children who have experienced traumatic situations, such as

---

[34]*From Child Growth and Development*, by Elizabeth B. Hurlock. © 1949, 1956, by McGraw-Hill. McGraw-Hill Book Company. Used by permission.
[35]Elizabeth B. Hurlock, *Ibid*, p. 326.

the loss of a loved-one through death or separation need as much reassurance that both the school and other members of their families can provide. Much can be done for them through busy, happiness-filled learning activities at school. A principal placed a little boy who had witnessed the death of his little sister, caused by a fire that destroyed the family's home, in a first-grade classroom where the needed emotional support could be provided, and the disturbed child could belong to a warm school family group.

Personality Traits

The early fostering of attractive personality traits in childhood is emphasized by Hurlock. Some of these traits and the recommendations for their development are listed below.

1. *Cheerfulness.* Hurlock listed three aids to the development of cheerfulness: A good, healthy condition, being surrounded by cheerful people, and the avoidance of all unnecessary restraints and frustrations.

2. *Enthusiasm.* Talking about, planning for, and anticipating the pleasure to come even from the simplest experiences, then at the time of the experience, emphasize the pleasant aspects and ignore the unpleasant aspects.

3. *A Sense of Humor.* Always encourage a young child to see the funny side of a difficult or irritating situation.

4. *Courage.* Instead of hovering over a child and showing concern for his safety, it is far better to do everything possible to see that his environment is safe and that his chances of hurting himself are reduced to the absolute minimum. Praise the child unstintingly for even a slight display of courage.

5. *Unselfishness.* Encouraging him to share his toys and possessions, in doing little kindnesses for others, and in making some contributions of his toys, clothes, or money to those less fortunate than he will go a long way toward focusing his attention toward others and away from himself. Unselfishness should be recognized.

6. *Sympathy.* Development of sympathy must wait upon the development of imagination, but, through careful direction, its development can be fostered slowly in the early years of childhood.

7. *Calmness*. Control the young child's environment so that there will be a minimum of exciting experiences. His room should be located in a quiet part of the house or apartment, and he should associate as much as possible with people who are calm.

8. *Self-confidence*. Hurlock listed these approaches to developing a child's self-confidence: Lavish praise for the child's efforts to do what is expected of him, give him plenty of opportunities to evaluate his abilities *favorably,* and teach the child to do things for himself as soon as he is capable of doing so.

9. *Self-assertiveness*. Give the child opportunities to assert himself within reason, when possible he may be given chances to state his preferences and to express himself on different matters.[36]

Language Development

Children need *many many* opportunities to learn to use words to express their meaning, to describe, answer questions, and to express their thoughts into verbal symbols. Those who are not ready to read obviously show this deficiency in ability to use verbal symbols.

A teacher of first graders observed that many of her students at the beginning of the year could not classify or tell why a series of pictures were similar or the way in which they were generally all alike. No child in the class could think of the word "uniform" when asked to tell what the suits of the pictured servicemen were called. When naming pictures projected onto the screen from filmstrips, only one student could think of the word "cot" to identify that picture. They could not tell what a cot is used for.

Parents who are alert for every possible opportunity to talk about daily experiences, identify new objects, and ask their child to tell how things are used together, where they may be found, in what ways some things are different, etc., can help to provide this supplementary help that is needed in language development.

The child's vocabulary is built through purposeful experiences and learning the names of things that are made meaningful through these experiences.

1. The names of farm and zoo animals can be introduced

---

[36]Elizabeth B. Hurlock, Ibid., pp. 327-336.

through visits to these places as well as by the use of picture books. Children can become aware of the sounds that farm animals make through direct experiences and records. Parents should provide these experiences as often as possible for their children, because even though such trips are often taken as culminating actitivities in unit studies at school, the school trips are not often enough or sufficient. Such experiences must be enjoyed over and over again. Children who have previously taken such trips often gain much more from the school studies because their experiences help them to be more aware of things to look for and to enjoy.

2. A scrapbook in which the child pastes pictures of farm animals in one section and zoo animals in another could be prepared by parent and child working together. Such pictures are abundant in coloring books and inexpensive picture books.

3. Pictures of mother animals could be matched with pictures of their babies. Much conversation between parent and child may be stimulated by these activities.

4. Parents may help their child to learn the names of garden tools, furniture, cooking utensils, and objects in the home. Many children who are found to be having difficulty with reading in the primary grades cannot name some of the pictured objects found in their workbooks. A child who cannot name a page of pictures cannot be ready to tell which ones rhyme or start with the same sound.

5. Trips to the supermarkets could be utilized to help the child learn the names of fruits and vegetables. This need not become a chore or an interference with the shopping. A casual, "This is the cauliflower. Cauliflower is a vegetable." or "Here are the strawberries. They are fruit" could be remarked to the child who is pushing the cart for his mother.

"Let's name all of the canned vegetables that we find on this shelf."

"We need corn. Here it is right by the peas."

"I see green beans here. What vegetable can you name?"

Classification

Children who cannot look at a group of pictures or objects and draw such general conclusions as (1) which are related or could go together for some reason; (2) which one is different from the others in purpose or other characteristics, and (3) what ways in which they may be alike and state these observations sufficiently in words will encounter difficulty later when they must read a chapter or other assignment and make conclusions concerning the reading material in addition to contending with the reading vocabulary. These children need additional help with classification and discussing and telling their reasons for grouping certain pictured objects together.

Games may be played by the parent and child in various interesting ways:

1. Using a picture dictionary or other similar picture book, the parent and child may take turns describing a picture on the page, such as, "I see something for work. It has wheels. What is it?" (Lawnmower.)

2. Pictures cut from magazines, catalogs, stamp premium catalogs, etc. can be used for such classifications as:

a. Things to be used in the living room, kitchen, kinds of food, eating utensils, things for work, etc.

b. Things for outdoor play.

c. Large or small toys.

d. Gardening tools, picnic supplies, things for camping, etc.

e. Finer classifications may be toys with wheels; things for mother or father; clothes or toys for babies, boys and girls; dishes or silverware or table settings, and furniture.

This classification of pictures may be done by pasting them in labeled sections on shelf paper.

Things for Father	*Things for Mother*
Toys with wheels	*Noisy toys*

The child will enjoy naming some of the pictures or using sentences to tell about or otewise describe them. Help may be given in formulating sentences by encouraging the child to tell about the pictures.

"This is a bicycle. It has wheels."

The parent and child may work together to make a shelf paper "cupboard" for the classification of pictured toys on "shelves." Shelves could be prepared for toys for a boy, those for a girl and things that a baby would like. Discussion between parent and child could motivate other incidental learnings as well as the classification skill.

"Let's put the tops on the *top* shelf."

"The baby's toys should be on the *bottom* shelf."

A similar "cupboard" could contain pictures of things that could be "put away" for Mother. The top shelf is for dishes, the middle for towels and washcloths, and the bottom is for pots, pans and other cooking utensils.

This activity can be repeated if the pictures are pinned to the shelves, placed in prepared slits or laid onto the paper cupboard if it is placed on the floor or other flat surface. The pictures may be pasted, also, but this would permit the activity of putting things on the shelves to be done only once with the need for the preparation of another "cupboard" if the activity is to be repeated. This classification activity could be varied to include the following:

1. A cupboard or workbench for Father's tools.

2. A cupboard for Mother with shelves for canned fruits and vegetables. If pictures of canned goods are not available, they could be outlined on paper and labeled, such as an outlined picture of a can of corn or peaches well labeled. The child can tell which shelf each can belongs on. This activity is a motivational one for the child's interest in helping in the home.

Making Associations

1. A "key" picture may be placed at the top of the page of construction or other paper. Three other pictures may be pasted below. The child then may be directed to find the picture below that is related to the top one.

Example: A picture of a pillow is at the top. Pictures of a stove, quilt and iron are below. The child is to choose the quilt, which is most associated with the pillow. In some cases, there may be more than one picture below that could be associated with the top one. The child then may tell his reason for his choice.

Making choices, giving reasons and associating related things are skills that are needed in evaluating reading content, and such comprehension abilities begin to grow in the preschool stage.

2. A large collection of pictures of furniture and other things that belong in the house could be collected from magazines, catalogs, etc. A long strip of shelf paper divided into sections may be labeled "The Kitchen," "The Living Room," "The Bedroom," etc. Parent and child may work together to paste, pin or otherwise classify each pictured item in its proper room.
"Here is the refrigerator. What room does it belong in?"
"Where does this sofa belong?"

In addition to the association and classification skills involved in this activity, the meaning of the printed words that are used in the labels will become real to the child. The experience of associating the printed words on the page of the reading book with real meaningful things in his daily living is necessary in reading readiness.

3. Matching things that are used together is possible in a variety of ways in the home. This can be done with real objects as well as through the use of pictures. Such objects as a key and lock, light bulb and lamp, needle and thread, etc. are examples of the numerous things in the home that can be used. A variety of things could be placed together for the child and parent to match as follows:
a. "Here is the key. What is it used with?"
b. Describing the object's use, such as, "I see something to use in sewing. What is it? What is it used with?"
c. "I see a light bulb. In what room is the thing that it is used with?" Telling the location of the object may be done as well as naming or describing it.
d. Matching pictures of foods that are usually eaten at breakfast, lunch and dinner may be done on shelf paper which is sectioned and labeled.

Auditory Discrimination

Reading requires skill in discriminating the sounds heard in words, listening for those that are different or similar, and sometimes using these sounds within words as aids in reading. Children can begin early to learn the listening skills and auditory discrimination. There is much that parents can do to help their child with this skill, too.

Early learning of purposeful listening will also do much to help the child grow in attention and interest abilities. Such skills do not just grow naturally, but must be learned through meaningful activities.

1. A variety of toys that make noise may be used such as: toy horns, animals that squeak, toy telephones, etc. Two of each kind of toy would make it possible to have one set in front of the child. The parent could place the other set where the child could not see them. After demonstrating with the set in front of the child to let him hear the sound that each toy makes the parent may say, "Now, I have some other toys just like these. Hide your eyes and listen. When a toy makes a noise, see if you can tell me which one made the noise."

2. The parent may read nursery rhymes to the child and talk about how some words rhyme. The child may listen for the rhyming words and raise his hand when he hears them. At first the parent may also indicate the rhyming words by hand raising. Later the child could do this by himself.

"Hey diddle, diddle, the cat and the fiddle." Hands are raised for *diddle, diddle* and *fiddle*. The parent could later read lines leaving out the rhyming words and ask the child to name them.

"Little Boy Blue, come blow your . . . . . The sheep are in the meadow, the cows in the . . ." The child says *horn* and *corn*.

The concept of rhyming words can be introduced by special emphasis in which the voice is raised and rhyming words are said louder when nursery rhymes are read to the child. "Humpty Dumpty sat on a WALL. Humpty Dumpty had a great FALL."

3. *Listening for Likenesses:* The child may be directed to listen for lines that are the same in rhymes.

"Mary had a *little lamb, little lamb, little lamb.*" The child may then repeat the refrains.

"Here we go 'round *the mulberry bush, the mulberry bush, the mulberry bush.*"

Finer Visual Discrimination

1. *Matching and Sorting:* (a) Inexpensive sets of marbles, small wooden beads or plastic Indian beads may be matched according to color or size. Containers such as small paper cups, egg cartons or small fruit or vegetable cartons could be used for this sorting activity. Broken strings of beads that are no longer useful may be used for sorting according to color, design or size. Sorting and matching of small objects also develops eye-hand coordination skill and increases the child's ability to work independently and see a task through to completion. Other things, such as plastic forks and spoons, buttons, and many others could be matched and sorted. (b) Matching small plastic toys, plastic numbers, letters or wooden blocks.

2. *Matching Likenesses:* (a) Inexpensive picture card sets or other small pictures may be used. One picture is to be placed at the top of the page and three including one like the top one are placed at the bottom. The child may be instructed to find and indicate the one at the bottom that is like the picture at the top. Composition books may be used for this activity. A different picture for each page should be prepared for the matching exercise.

Stencils involving various shapes may be matched in the above described way. A shape is placed at the top of the page and its corresponding one is at the bottom with others and is to be identified and indicated (Fig. 34).

(b) Cottage cheese or similar containers may be used for the sorting or matching of mosaic tiles according to size, shape, design or color. A "key" tile (the one to guide the child in matching all others like it) may be glued to the bottom or at the top of the container, and the child is instructed to place the matching tiles in each container. Two or three children may work together, or the child may do this with a parent or by himself.

(c) Floral, bird and animal seals can be glued in carton lids such as those for ice cream, etc. Matching seals may be glued to cardboard discs. The child may match the seals by placing

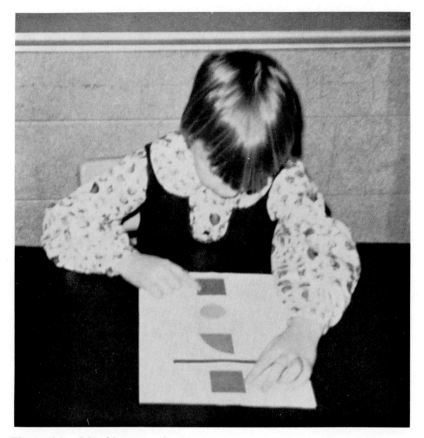

Figure 34. Matching stencils.

the corresponding cardboard discs in the lid with the similar seal.

(d) *Color matching* can be done in various ways, such as:

Baking cups can be matched or grouped according to color, or they could be held up individually as the child is asked to find matching ones.

Colored hors d'oeuvre sticks or toothpicks can be matched or grouped.

Plastic numbers or alphabet blocks may be matched.

Colored pipe cleaners or chenille wires may be matched according to color or length.

Designs may be marked on wooden spoons with felt marking pens. Children may match the designs that are alike.

Gummed stars or letters may be placed on wooden spoons, the bottoms of nut cups, etc. and they may be matched.

(e) *Letter Matching.* Letters may be pasted to the nut cup bottoms. The children may place the two nut cups together and show how they match.

Plastic letters or those from stencil books may be matched.

Letters may be arranged in rows so that there is one placed first in the row with various others plus some like the first one. The child may be instructed to find all of the letters like the first one.

(f) *Button Matching.* Buttons of various sizes may be collected. Large colorful ones may be matched in pairs for likenesses in color, shape and design. The children may later match small ones.

Rows may be prepared for the children to find all of the buttons that are alike.

Buttons may be used for children to find the one that is different. This exercise may progress from the very easy to the difficult. Three buttons that are alike and one that is different may be glued to a card or other surface. The child may point to the one that is different on each card.

Making Comparisons

1. (a) *Bigger and Smaller.* Buttons of two sizes may be glued to cards. The child may be asked to point to the smaller or larger button.

(b) Buttons of three sizes may be used for small, larger and largest. The parent may ask the child to find the larger one, then comparisons may be made of the various sizes.

"Here is the small one. Is this other one larger or smaller than this one?" (Cover up the largest one.)

"Now, which one is the larger of these two?" (Point to the buttons.) "Which of these is larger?"

2. *Longer and Longest.* (a) Real objects such as a ruler, and a pencil, etc., may be used. "Which is long?" "Which is short?"

(b) Three objects on the card. Compare the lengths. "Is

the pencil longer or shorter than the ruler?" (Cover up the pencil.) "Is the ruler longer or shorter than the pen?"

3. *First and Last.* (a) Three plastic spoons, buttons, etc. of different colors may be prepared. The child may be asked what color the *first* one is, the *last,* etc.

(b) Introduce the *middle* one.

(c) *Ordinal*—first, second, third, fourth, fifth, etc, may be introduced through the use of three dimensional objects, etc.

Preschool Summer Program

The readiness activities described in this section were prepared and used in a summer program for preschool children. These summer school classes were held at the home of one of the children. Parents attended the classes to observe, and the mother at whose home the classes were held assisted the teacher.

The purpose of the summer school program was to plan and devise techniques and instructional materials that parents could use at home with their preschool children. The aim was also to help parents more fully realize what is involved in reading readiness and to help them to participate in the preventive aspect of school readiness preparation.

Through helping parents to realize how readiness involves many experiences that begin very early in the child's life, the parental desire to help can be used to share in the child's readiness preparation and to supplement his school instruction more effectively. The interest and support of a child's parents through his school life contributes greatly to his success and security, and the effectiveness of this support can be improved through better communication and understanding of the school curriculum as interpreted by the school personnel to the parents.

Twelve children participated in the program. The interest remained high throughout the summer. The children attended the classes three times a week, each session lasting one hour, and occasionally fifteen or twenty minutes beyond that length of time.

The preschoolers were very proud and eager to do well when their mothers visited the classes. Parents reported that their children were interested and eager to attend. One child's mother informed the teacher that he got up at five o'clock one morning announcing that he wished to try to make it hurry up and be two o'clock so that he could go to school.

The children gained in ability to do the manipulative activities, and became very skillful in the ability to see likenesses and differences in very fine and internal detail. They learned to match likenesses in various objects. The interest and attention span increased to the extent that they were always working eagerly at the end of each session. There were never any such statements to indicate lack of interest or the desire to go home before the end of the class session.

They were very kind and patient as they waited for someone to have his turn. There was a desire to be helpful through courtesy shown by not interrupting or being critical of the efforts of each other. They listened to their classmates. There was much enthusiasm, and the teacher enjoyed the summer school very much as well as the children and their parents.

Recommendations

This type of preschool program could be held by parents. The children who attended this school in a parent's home lived close enough in the neighborhood so that there was no transportation problem. Parents may easily work together in a neighborhood and have a similar type of program involving the readiness activities and techniques described in this section. High-school students who are participating in the Cadet Teacher program could, through the guidance of their sponsoring teachers, assist parents in such preschool readiness programs as the one described herein. It seems that this would be a worthy effort.

Special sessions are needed with the parents of all preschool children as early as possible, two or three years before the children start school, for demonstrations of techniques to be used with helping the child to prepare for school. Suggestions are needed regarding the ways in which parents may more fully participate in their child's readiness preparation before the school entrance. The earlier that parents realize how much they can contribute to their child's successful school voyage, the more can be accomplished toward *prevention* of storms or at least the recognition of their danger signals.

To cooperate effectively with the school in the furtherance of the reading program, parents need certain specific information which must be available at the right time. If given too late, as when a child has been placed in the not-ready-to-read group in a readiness program, the parent is often placed in an adverse position and is in a poor frame of mind to receive suggestions. [37]

Parents can accept the need to not expose their child to formal reading until he is ready if they understand the importance of the readiness program, what the school is doing to help, and what they can do to contribute to the solving of the learning problem, thus providing for the child's later reading success.

"Oh, if I had just known this six years ago!" parents have often said after they were helped to fully understand the importance of readiness skill development.

Parental Participation

The amount of parent involvement in the school program varies, and while in some schools parents may work actively in the parent-teacher activities of their local association, they may do little participation of the kind relating to classroom activities. Other schools may encourage more parental help in the classroom activities. More encouragement of parents to share in the school activities can provide for their understanding of their possible contribution to school readiness.

Some school systems go beyond welcoming visiting parents and invite them to actively participate in carrying on school activities. This has a two-fold purpose: (1) to acquaint the parents with the school and all of its activities and problems, and (2) to utilize parent talents for the benefit of the school.

The type of participation in the schools that invite it varies all the way from asking the parents to do mainly clerical work to having them give actual help in the classroom.[38]

It seems very necessary for parents to become more involved in the actual school day activities of their children. More worth-

[37]From *Reading in Your School,* by Roy J. Newton, © 1960, by McGraw-Hill Book Company. Used by permission of the Publishers.

[38]From Grace Langdon and Irving W. Stout *Teaching in the Primary Grades,* © 1964, p. 438. Courtesy of the MacMillan Company, New York, Collier-MacMillan

while evaluation of the schools and suggestions can be made by those who have shared the experiences and their planning. Parents need to more fully realize the instructional aims of the school and understand why progress may be slow for some students, and become more aware of effort directed toward remedying the discrepancies between what is realized as needed and what attempt is being made to accomplish this need. Parents can become more aware of the complexities of learning skills and the constant need for effort to devise ways and materials to meet pupil needs. They can realize how enormous is the task of meeting the needs of the other students who are so much like yet so different in needs, abilities and experiences from their own little Joe. They can become so much a part of the program and planning that they will share the joys and hopes for the progress of others in the class as well as these for Joe.

Familiarity with the school routine can be helpful to parents in knowing their own child better through the many opportunities to see him work and play with other children. This will enable the parent, who knows more about his own child and his world outside the school than anyone else, and the teacher, who is prepared to interpret his needs as realized through his participation with a group of children, to better understand each other's role as well as to view one's own in a more complete perspective. The parents will understand how their child functions with the group, how he is like yet different from others, and how participation with a group influences him.

Parents may participate in the school program in many ways. Some possibilities are as follows:

1. Arrangements may be made with those parents who can spend a day in the classroom occasionally. They may serve as teachers' aids helping the children with seatwork or individual activities or give other help as directed by the teacher.

2. Parent workshop periods may be planned during which the teacher may direct parents in helping with the preparation of charts or other instructional materials. Parents may also prepare such additional instructional devices for use with supplementary work with their child at home to reinforce what is being done at school.

3. Grandmothers or other relatives who may be retired teachers may enjoy coming to school and helping occasionally. A little boy's grandmother who visited school one day and was invited by the teacher to help the children with seatwork activities happily remarked at the end of the day, "This is the most wonderful visit I ever had at school!" She had been a teacher's aide as well as her grandson's visitor during this Open House week.

4. Special "open house" days may be planned during which parents may come and spend an hour or two working with their children on seatwork projects or with other materials. Many "Open House" activities during American Education Week involve observations by parents of their children's work as displayed on bulletin boards, but if more definite planning is done, there is also visitation during school hours when there can be observation of the school's most important product — the children in action.

Early Vision Evaluation

The seriousness of a preschool child's possible visual difficulty and suggestions for helping parents to recognize symptoms that possibly indicate the need for the child's vision to be evaluated by an ophthalmologist are offered by Doctor Jules H. Shaw who practices ophthalmology in Boston, Massachusetts. Doctor Shaw emphasized the fact that it is just as important for parents of preschool children as it is for parents of school children to be aware of symptoms that indicate possible eye difficulties.

Doctor Shaw recommends that all children be given an ophthalmological examination first at the age of three unless symptoms appear before this age. His recommended testing program includes a complete series of eye screening tests for visual acuity, excessive farsightedness, and eye muscle imbalance.

According to Doctor Shaw, some behavior patterns that suggest the need for an eye examination are listed below:

1. The child may attempt to brush away blur.
2. He may frown or rub his eyes excessively.
3. He may shut or close one eye, tilt his head or throw it forward when looking at near or distant objects.

4. Perhaps he has difficulty in reading or coloring; he stumbles or trips over small objects.

5. He may hold a book or small object close to his eyes.

6. He may be unable to participate in games requiring distance vision.

7. He may be unduly sensitive to light, have red rimmed, encrusted or swollen eyelids, recurring sties, or inflamed or watering eyes.

8. Crossed eyes, dizziness, headaches or nausea at close work, and/or double vision are additional indications that something is wrong.

The earlier faulty vision is corrected, the better.[39]

Early Medical Examination

Other aspects of the child's health including adequate medical checkups, dental care and provision for special health needs of the individual child are significant to developing readiness for learning. Parents who also instruct their child in the early development of worthwhile health habits, self-care and good eating habits contribute greatly to his preparation for school.

The material contained in this section concerns some ways in which parents can share in their child's growth in reading readiness. The purpose is not to glibly "tell parents what they ought to do," but to share ideas, foster understanding, and to interpret goals of both teacher and parent as they strive to meet the needs of the child.

Other Parental Needs for Help

There are children whose parents cannot run to the corner five and ten-cent store and purchase even the inexpensive items described herein. Due to many circumstances, there may not be the money or time available for the parents to utilize these techniques and materials for the preparation of their children for school readiness.

There are many homes where there is only one parent who must work to support the family as well as attempt to assume both

---

[39]From Jules Harold Shaw, M.D.: Vision and seeing skills of preschool children. *The Reading Teacher,* October, 1964, pp. 35-6. Reprinted with permission of Jules Harold Shaw and the International Reading Association.

parental responsibilities. In some homes, both parents may be working, but still there are only the bare essentials and no extra little comforts that are taken for granted by many other children. The children in these homes may not have ever gone to the zoo, the circus or the library. There is no rich background of experiences for these children to draw from as they learn to read. According to Catherine Brunner, project coordinator Early School Admissions Project in the Baltimore Public Schools, in describing the research-based experimental project for four-year-olds begun in 1962, many children when they first came to the project did not know their own names. They are often referred to at home as "little sister" or "little boy."

> Some children do not know how they look, for they have seldom looked at themselves in a mirror or seen photographs of themselves.[40]

The growing national concern for the plight of such children as those who live in the coal mining areas, Appalachia, Harlem or Hastings Street in Detroit, Michigan, as well as both city and rural slum areas has motivated an all-out war against poverty and its effects upon the learning abilities of children.

The realization that this is everybody's problem to solve has been brought home to the President, legislators, educators and all who are interested in the needs of children. Researchers are beginning to define the learning needs of the disadvantaged children and determine the extent of their handicaps. Problem-solving has been approached through consideration of family and pupil needs, different kinds of deprivation and their influences upon the child, teacher education and understanding of the unique needs of these handicapped learners, and evaluation of instructional materials and techniques.

The Economic Opportunity Act of 1964 has made provisions for the following:

1. **The Job Corps**—Men and women between the ages of sixteen through twenty-one may participate in an ungraded

---

[40]From Catherine Brunner, More than an ounce of prevention. *Childhood Education,* September, 1965, p. 37. Courtesy of the *Journal of the Association for Childhood Education International,* 3615 Wisconsin Avenue, N.W., Washington, D.C. (20016).

basic education and job skill training program.

2. **The Neighborhood Youth Corps**—Will provide part-time employment and job training for young men in their own home-towns.

3. An adult basic education program for persons over eighteen who have not completed elementary school.

4. Low-cost, long-term loans will be extended to rural families.

5. For small businesses, inexpensive loans of up to $25,000 are being made available to help existing businesses and in the establishment of others.

6. Work-experience programs to provide vocational training for heads of families who need this help to become employable.

7. Grants and loans to states, local communities, and special non-profit organizations for the establishment of housing, education, sanitation, personal hygiene and child care programs for migrant agricultural workers and their families.

8. VISTA—**Volunteers in Service to America** is a domestic version of the Peace Corps. Within a year, 3,500 or more Americans will have the opportunity to volunteer to help in the struggle. Some Volunteers are already living and working with the poor—in city and rural slums, on Indian reservations, in mental hospitals, with migrant workers, in Job Corps Centers, and in other federal, state and community anti-poverty programs.[41]

"Project Head Start" programs are sponsored by the Economic Opportunity Act, also. These community operated six-to-eight-week summer sessions of preschool education for four- and five-year-old children from disadvantaged homes are for the purpose of giving these children a chance to adjust to the world outside their limited environment, improve their health and language skills, and "catch up" with youth of average background.[42]

Vernon F. Haubrich, who as an associate professor at Hunter College worked on a project to prepare young prospective teachers for service in disadvantaged areas of East Harlem and is now Associate Professor in the Department of Curriculum and Teaching

[41]From Morton R. Engelberg: The other America. *The Michigan Education Journal,* March, 1965, Vol. 42, pp. 9-10. Courtesy of The Michigan Education Association.
[42]"Project Head Start," From What's ahead for Michigan? *Michigan Education Journal,* May, 1965, Vol. 42, No. 19, p. 65. Courtesy of The Michigan Education Association Lansing, Michigan.

at Teachers College, Columbia University, emphasized the need for the beginning or experienced teacher to be equipped with the following skills which are absolutely essential for success in schools serving disadvantaged or depressed areas:

1. The ability to understand and utilize developmental and remedial reading procedures.
2. The ability to organize and routinize specific classroom procedures.
3. The ability to reconstruct syllabi, textbooks, and reading materials in terms of the background of students.
4. The ability to work effectively with small groups within the classroom and to know when to use such procedure.
5. The ability to adjust new entrants to the classroom situation quickly.
6. The ability to construct and use concrete materials for classroom work.
7. The ability to handle aggression and violence.
8. The ability to use individual and group procedures in gaining classroom discipline.
9. The ability to know when a child should be referred and to whom.
10. A knowledge of the language pattern in the area and the ability to correct such patterns.
11. A knowledge of neighborhood and family to see what effect this has on classroom work and procedures.
12. The ability to translate the "academic" knowledge of children from depressed areas into specific procedures for classroom use.[43]

Individual school districts have accomplished much in the realization and evaluation of pupils needs and in the adjustment and preparation of curriculum materials accordingly.

Detroit, Michigan Public Schools, representing children of multicultural backgrounds with needs to be more adequately provided for through reading materials involving stories depicting life situations more similar to their own, prepared a special reading

---

[43]From Vernon F. Haubrich: The culturally disadvantaged and teacher education. *The Reading Teacher*, March, 1965, Vol. 18 No. 6, pp. 502-503. Reprinted with permission of Vernon F. Haubrich and the International Reading Association, Newark, Delaware.

program for the urban schools. This project began in 1959 as part of the Great City School Improvement Program in Detroit, and the Writers' Committee, under the chairmanship of Gertrude Whipple, developed the reading materials for boys and girls who live in multicultural cities. These reading materials are published by Follett Publishing Company.

The reading texts of the Detroit Public Schools include stories and pictorial illustrations of Negro and white children working and playing together, visiting each other in their homes, and sharing other experiences. This preparation of special curriculum materials to meet special needs eliminated the reading of texts picturing children of one race only with content and concepts relating only to middle-class experiences not shared and understood by the readers.

Current research concerning the disadvantaged child supports the hypothesis that the children must be reached and helped through extensive pre-kindergarten programs. This is why the programs are called "Head Start." The effort is aimed at giving them a head start through preventive instruction that will eliminate their learning handicaps surely to result if children are not reached in the preschool years.

Special Needs

Many first-grade classrooms, even those that are not located in what are considered deprived areas, have some experience-deprived children. These few children may not ever have been to a zoo, a farm, airport, or may otherwise be limited in experiences. Plans of educators to meet the needs of deprived children must include these children. The close cooperation of parents and teachers, as well as more interpretation of the importance of the experiential background in readiness preparation may motivate more parental provision of trips, activities for readiness that can be accomplished at home and talking with their children and answering their questions, but effort and use of funds allocated for disadvantaged children need to be directed toward the needs of these few children, also. More provision for school bus trips to enable the children to gain through the direct purposeful experiences of field trips, and the purchase of more audiovisual equipment for schools are possible means through which a contribution can be made to meeting the need.

The meaning of "deprived" or "disadvantaged" may not necessarily apply to economic status only. Some children may have an abundance of toys and other luxuries, but may be deprived of the companionship and needed attention of parents or others. A child who has an abundance of toys but has not been taught to care for them or put them away after play is deprived. A boy who attended a summer school remedial program seemed to need much emotional support and help. Both parents were working, and since this boy was much younger than his teen-age brothers, he really had little companionship within his family. Children need the support and companionship of adults in addition to that of their peers. This boy's family was well within the middle-class economic range, but he was a disadvantaged child deprived of needed emotional support and help. The teacher observed many indications of his need during his attendance in summer school classes.

Some children may be deprived of toys and other material advantages, but may live where there are few restrictions or dangers associated with their play. They may be able to enjoy long walks or camping trips into the woods to see and hear bird life, learn about wild flowers, observe the stages in the life cycle of a frog in nearby ponds, be able to own and care for an abundance of pets, or learn by seeing which snakes they need not fear. They may have the opportunity to watch a mother blue jay teach her youngster to fly, and they may watch the step-by-step building of a wren's nest in a house that was built by themselves with the help of a parent. Such are priceless background experiences that may be enjoyed by children who may live where they are possible.

Children are also deprived for the following reasons:

1. Live in an area where there are too many dangers or reasons to cause them to be fearful.

2. Are not permitted to make choices or their own decisions within reasonable limits.

3. Are not permitted to explore or seek ways to express their own creativity.

4. Haven't learned to play with others without always having their own way.

5. Have never or rarely been read to or introduced to the wonderful world of good stories.

6. Never have learned to accept the fact that they have made a mistake.

7. Can't share with others.

8. Can't find anything to do if the television is out of order or they are alone.

9. Rarely can feel that their contributions or efforts are worthwhile.

10. Have too many restrictions placed upon their choice of friends.

11. Cannot feel confident about their own adequacy as a person; feel too anxious, ill at ease or cannot make friends.

12. Cannot understand or sympathize with the feelings of others.

13. Have no parent or other adult whom they can relate with and emulate.

14. Do not have some older persons as their friends as well as those their same age or younger.

15. Have not been taught to be kind to animals.

16. Have been too protected so that they fear all new situations, cry before there is an apparent reason to feel afraid or hurt.

17. Do not have the opportunity to enjoy the companionship of their parents or others in their family.

The effort to understand the unique learning handicaps of the disadvantaged children will demand careful consideration, research, and evaluation. The efforts to help the large groups of children in whole depressed areas must also be supplemented by individual teacher research in classrooms anywhere that contain a child who has been deprived of experiences necessary to aid learning. Without such teacher interest, the program cannot succeed, no matter how large may be the amount of government—allocated funds.

Parental interest and participation in their child's readiness for reading and school success are necessary regardless of the family economic status. The need exists for greater and more effective communication between school and home years before the child enters the school classroom. Reading readiness is a major factor in the child's school program, and the parent's contribution may be what determines success or failure for the child as well as what is done for him in school.

The material contained in this section has been a presentation of some ways in which many parents can help to prepare their child for reading readiness. The next section will concern the disadvantaged child, his unique learning needs, and some ways in which he can be helped to gain vocabulary concepts, an experiential background and sensory experiences. Some possible ways in which this child's parents can help will also be presented.

Chapter X

READINESS ACTIVITIES FOR THE DISADVANTAGED CHILD

T HE VOCABULARY OF MEANINGS, understanding of concepts and experiential background so vital to readiness for reading are extremely limited for the disadvantaged children. The needs of these children are becoming the subject for much needed research by educators.

The adverse effects of deprivation upon a child's ability to learn is a growing concern of educators as they are continually being revealed through efforts to evaluate learning abilities, understand certain handicaps and seek instructional techniques to meet the individual needs of each child. Evidences of this concern are apparent in articles containing theories and research findings that support the hypotheses suggesting that for best results, the children of the slums must be reached through extensive pre-kindergarten facilities and programs.

Levine stressed the fact that social conditions tend to perpetuate themselves and thus causing children who have experienced little but deprivation and violence to become "the walking wounded" of the next generation. His suggested solutions are as follows:

1. Changing the forces that drive experienced and competent teachers to the wealthiest school systems, leaving those children with the greatest need under the care of beginning transient instructors.
2. Working closely with the parents of culturally deprived children.
3. Special remedial services for children with disadvantaged backgrounds.
4. The most important: "But even beyond these valid and useful suggestions we need to attack the problem at its source—the experience and conditioning of the preschool years. By the

time a child from a deprived environment reaches school, his development is already determined to a degree that makes it nearly impossible for the school to grant him full educational opportunity." [44]

Mrs. Brunner described the research-based experimental project for four-year-olds begun in 1962 and jointly financed by the Baltimore City Public Schools and the Ford Foundation. The author cited this example of problems caused by conditions in the depressed areas:

> *Retardation in Learning.* The program of the Baltimore Project is directed toward determining whether early admission to school can overcome any of the barriers to learning which environmental factors seem to impose. This educational program designed to enrich the lives of four-year-old children who require compensating educational services is designed to discover ways to:
>
> (a) Accelerate the achievement of children limited in their development by environmental factors beyond their control.
>
> (b) Increase parental understanding of the values of education and to increase the degree to which parents accept the responsibility for the education of their children.
>
> (c) Facilitate communication between the school and community agencies as they work together to assist children and adults in depressed areas in attempting to raise their aspirations and improve their levels of competence. [45]

Many challenges will continue to confront the educators who wish to help the disadvantaged. This effort will require understanding of the child's culture and way of life, how it influences his attitudes, and a fuller realization of what this child's family considers important in life, and parental ambitions for the child.

According to Olsen, while it is true that deprivation is one major aspect of the lower-income culture, its significance has been overemphasized. He believes that it is necessary to face the fact that lower-class children are socialized in ways that are quite different from those of the middle class. Full account must be taken

---

[44]From Daniel U. Levine: City schools today: Too late with too little. *Phi Delta Kappan,* Nov. 1962, p. 82. Courtesy of Phi Delta Kappa, Inc., Spencer, Indiana.

[45]From Catherine Brunner, *loc. cit.,* pp. 35-6.

of the different value patterns, attitudes, and beliefs with which the lower-class child comes to school.

> The child brings the reality of his own life into the classroom, and to be effective the school must admit that reality.[46]

Olsen suggests that the central challenge presented by the slum child to the school is not only his disadvantages, but also his ambition, hopes, desires, his attitude toward authority, education, success, and school, his fears, his habits, his hates—his basic orientation toward life—are in many ways, so different from ours that we do not understand him nor does he understand us.[47]

It is important for educators to not assume that merely because a child's culture is *different* that he is necessarily culturally *deprived*. A child may share a rich cultural heritage within his family, yet be handicapped at school or in the community because he lives where this heritage is not shared or understood by others. The school must provide for this special learning need. The Spanish-speaking child whose parents are farm laborers may possess cultural experiences that he can share with his classmates in various ways in correlation with school activities. His parents may be invited to come to their child's school and show keepsakes or souvenirs from their home country. Children from other countries may encourage their parents to prepare a type of food for the class that is representative of their country in correlation with a social studies project. Handwork, pottery or other family treasures that the parents may be able to show their child's classmates offer the opportunity for *sharing* their culture.

A first grader at Maplewood School in Garden City, Michigan, was so proud of the fact that her mother held her class in rapt attention as she described Christmas in Germany during a special sharing time.

Mrs. Alta Ford, teacher at Preston School in Detroit, Michigan, remarked one day after receiving big, shiny apples from her students, "Oh, I have so many apples that I will have to make some baked apples tonight."

---

[46]From James Olsen: Challenge of the poor to the schools. *Phi Delta Kappan,* November, 1962, p. 79. Courtesy of Phi Delta Kappa, Inc.

[47]James Olsen, *Ibid.,* p. 79.

One of her Spanish-speaking students asked, "How do you make a baked apple, Mrs. Ford?"

His teacher described the steps involved in baked apple preparation, and the fourth grade boy went home during the lunch period and helped his mother prepare baked apples. He proudly brought some to school that afternoon. Undoubtedly the boy's family ate baked apples for dessert very often thereafter!

Mrs. Ford's students present a program during their annual Piñata party and share their songs and customs with the other students and friends. Parents help in the preparation of the Piñatas. The involvement of parents in the school program is as important, if not more so, in regard to the disadvantaged child than it is for any child. These parents need encouragement and guidance in the realization that their contributions to their child's school program are indispensable. Too often it is assumed that these parents do not care or are not interested in becoming involved in the school program. They care, but effort must be put forth to improve communication between home and school and to interpret school aims and goals. The parent who realizes that the curriculum goals are meaningful and purposeful in life will be willing to help.

Asbell describes how a major part of preschool experimentation has been done to find ways of teaching parents how to help. Ways in which parents have been involved were cited as follows:

1. Many cities with new preschool centers require as a "tuition fee" for the child, that the impoverished mother attend weekly classes in the physical and cognitive development of children.

2. Mothers may serve as teachers' aides.

3. At Ypsilanti, Michigan, Dr. Weikart's preschool teachers make a home visit every afternoon ostensibly to report to parents on a child's progress. But the visit is mostly taken up with engaging the mother, the preschool pupil and perhaps half a dozen brothers and sisters in games, story reading, working with crayons and paper, thus encouraging the delighted mother to become a preschool teacher herself in her own home.[48]

---

[48]From Bernard Asbell: Six years old is too late. *Redbook*, September, 1965, p. 128. Courtesy of McCall Corporation, 230 Park Ave. New York 17, N.Y.

Doctor Robert Hess, chairman of the University of Chicago's Committee on Human Development, is questioning and searching possibilities for ways in which the mother's attitude and treatment may affect the child's intake and sorting of information, and the development of learning patterns. Doctor Hess's staff is conducting research concerning mother-child relations, and the pattern is emerging that the impoverished mother introduces her children to much the same world she found. This research is being done with several impoverished Negro families, as well as in contrasting middle-class ones.[49]

Much research will continue to be done regarding parental influences upon their children. Possibly Doctor Hess has presented a research contribution that will be a guideline to be followed in continued research programs involving large numbers of children and families representative of other sections of the country and nationalities, also.

Long-range and follow-up studies to evaluate educational measures are needed for the disadvantaged child as well as research involving social factors. This type of research will be needed to evaluate the head start and remedial instructional programs. Much information is being gleaned from research studies in all aspects of the disadvantaged child's life.

The purpose of this review of research and theory has been to present some of the broad areas necessary to be explored in regard to the needs of the disadvantaged child. The concern is primarily an educational one, but the all-out effort to help this child requires identifying the causes and sources for his learning handicaps, and applying both preventive and corrective measures in the home, school and other aspects of his life.

Disadvantaged children lack the experiential background that is needed to prepare them for the skills involved in reading. The "behind-the-scenes" activities that are automatically participated in by the advantaged child are lacking in the life of the culturally deprived student. If the disadvantaged child is exposed to any other readiness program than one that provides for his unique learning handicaps, it is apparent that he is not ready for the pre-

---

[49]Bernard Asbell, *Ibid.*, p. 126.

reading activities directly related to formal reading, and should not be exposed to these skills until special provision has been made for these needs.

The readiness program for the disadvantaged child must include lesson planning with aims directed toward providing the actual direct experiences first, then much repetition of skill introduction based upon these experiences and reintroduced through a variety of meaningful and interesting media. These media must include audiovisual aids, sensory experiences, teacher-pupil participation in discussions to evaluate, compare, observe, listen, ask, answer, classify, and share many other experiences that these children have not previously been motivated or permitted to do.

This writing consists of the effort to consider some of the needs of the disadvantaged preschool child, consider his readiness needs, utilize some supportive research or observations, and to suggest some possible workable and meaningful readiness instructional activities and techniques for helping this student. Every effort to evaluate and provide for this need may possibly make some contribution to the growth of awareness and realization of what the schools can do for this learner whose needs are so unique.

Strom reported some of the psychological consequences likely to occur in crowded living conditions as follows:

> . . . lack of self-sufficiency, destruction of illusions, mental strain, and the inability to make decisions.[50]
> Persistent crowding from early life seems to affect adversely the self-sufficiency of slum children, their ability to be alone, and their individuality.[51]

Readiness activities to help the child who has suffered from the above conditions must reflect an awareness of the learner's limitations as well as the instructional goals involved. The student who cannot function without the emotional support of others around him constantly, yet needs to develop self-sufficiency should be provided with a variety of interesting things that he can do by himself, yet also be near others if he chooses. The tasks to be done

---

[50]From Robert D. Strom: *Teaching in The Slum School.* © 1965, p. 5. Courtesy of Charles E. Merrill Books Inc., 1300 Alum Creek Drive, Columbus, Ohio.
[51]Robert D. Strom, *Ibid.,* p. 5.

individually must be easy enough to insure his immediate success, because the initial aim is to develop his self-confidence. Later, challenge should be presented only in accordance with his growth in skills and abilities.

It seems that tasks for the child who lacks ability in so many skill areas must be provided through lesson planning based upon specific skill developmental aims. Each task or lesson to be introduced should possibly include only one aim, and provision for sequential introduction of skills should be permitted. The child who has fairly well mastered simple coloring, but can accomplish only gross use of scissors should perhaps be expected to do independently only part of an art project involving both of these skills and then have individual help by the teacher to complete the rest of the activity.

The planning of projects or activities, especially those for art or handicraft sometimes necessarily involves those which require supplementary skills in addition to the one for which the lesson is aimed, but needed individual help must be available for the child who has so many skills to master.

The pupil who is striving to become aware of his own individuality or needs guidance to foster this growth needs to experience many concrete evidences of himself as a person. These may be provided in many possible ways including frequent use of his name in relationship to his work, possessions, and his other contributions to the group effort.

> Today, let's listen again to the record that Joe likes so well.
> Mary chose this story book from the library shelf. Let's listen to Mary's story.
> Look, Bill, this is your name on your locker. This locker is just for your things.

Frequent use of the children's names, writing something on their papers to express what they feel should be said to describe their art activities, use of photographs or slides relating to the children and their experiences, frequent showing or displaying these pictures, expressing happiness when a child returns to school after an absence, sending get-well cards to those who are ill, and many other small but important personal attentions can contribute to the child's realization of his worth as a person.

The children need opportunities to have privacy if they wish the occasional chance to be alone. A boy whose family totaled eighteen, including two married sisters with children, was cooperative and willing to share in group games, but during free play time, he was usually over by the large window ledge "flying" his toy plane by himself or watching for trucks and his other favorite vehicles on the road. He seemed to need this time to be alone and enjoy his solitude. He loved to share his things with the other children, but at other times he needed to be by himself.

The detrimental effect of crowding upon the development of decision-making abilities cited by Strom would contribute to the retardation of reading readiness abilities. The child who lacks the ability to make even the simplest decisions needs much help to grow in this ability. Some possible readiness activities to help overcome this handicap are listed below:

1. Giving the child the chance to choose which toy, story book or game he wishes to play, but at first the possible choices should be very few in number, such as two things to choose from, then later three, etc. Too many choices without the needed help to use them will only confuse the child.

2. Games to be played with a few children and opportunities for choices concerning which child will be "It" next, objects in the room to be used in the game, etc.

3. Choices in which there is no "right" or "wrong" answer, but whatever the child may say is an acceptable response. Example: "Which of these two pictures do you like best?" "Which of these colors do you think is the prettiest?"

4. Grossly easy examples of which the correct one is very obvious. Example: A very large and a very small ball. The child is asked, "Which is the big one?"

The children need to have immediate success in their first attempts at decision-making. They need much encouragement and frequent opportunities to express their ideas, and if their contributions are met with criticism before they have sufficient self-confidence to accept this, they will withdraw and say nothing. It is easier to not answer or say, "I don't know," than to risk disapproval, especially from one's classmates. The teacher's attitude very frequently influences the students, and this determines whether or not the group atmosphere is conducive to individual spontaneous expression of ideas. Perhaps many students have rarely or never been asked, "What do you think?" Questions such as this when followed by interested listening to their ideas aid the development of self-confidence. The children who are discouraged at home in their attempts to talk or ask questions need this extra help and attention at school.

Readiness includes a broad background in concepts that has been gained through real experiences involving seeing, handling, tasting, hearing, receiving information from adult explanations, being listened to, having one's questions answered, and through every possible way in which one can participate both actually and vicariously. The disadvantaged child, who has such a limited experiential background, must have this lack provided for through his school program. Time and special lesson planning relating to these needs are necessary.

The vocabulary section to follow will deal with some areas in which concepts can be built through readiness activities and experiences. The skills involved and the conceptual vocabulary meanings will be included with each suggested example.

Although real experiences are the best instructional avenues, and use of pictures, filmstrips and other visual aids contribute to the effectiveness of this first-hand experience, these may be used interchangeably. For example, use of pictures and more abstract devices may be effective for introductory purposes. Pictures of fruits and vegetables may be shown in correlation with their being eaten in the classroom, then later they may be used for review and vocabulary development activities in which the children name them.

The examples to be described are only a few suggestions that begin with some of the most basic self-care needs, the child's self-awareness and recognition of familiar objects, animals, foods, and things that are usually used in the preschool child's home and neighborhood. These are some of the first steps upon which there must be a continual building of concepts. The child's vocabulary and other aspects of readiness are continuous and require constant provision for growth.

I. Self-care Skills

    A. *Skill:* Learning to dress properly for cold weather.

    B. *Activities:* Dressing self for outdoor play.
Reinforcement activity of pretending to dress a doll for outdoor play.

    C. *Vocabulary:* (Possible new concepts.)

        1. Coat, snowsuit, hat, cap, scarf, hood, boots, rubbers, overshoes, galoshes, leggings, ski pants, button, un-button, zip, zipper, put on, take off, hang up, wear, un-zip, tie, untie, mittens, gloves, head, arms, fingers, hands, feet, body, sleeves, cold, windy, snowy, icy, blustery, etc.

        2. The above concepts may be more fully understood by the child as they are used in conversation or in other activities in correlation with the learning of the self-care skill of dressing for outdoor play.

    D. *Supplementary Activities:*
Viewing and talking about filmstrips or films in which people are dressed for cold weather.
Pictures from magazines may be collected and utilized for observation of those that include cold weather activities or people dressed for outdoors. They may be classified or otherwise discussed and used in teacher and pupil class work.

    E. *Language Development:*

        1. Games may be played for which the children ask questions or name something to be indicated by another child. Example: "I see a girl with her boots on. Who can find her?" Rules of the game may include an effort to answer in a sentence, such as, "Here is the girl with her boots on."

        Much help from the teacher will be needed in addition to use of a variety of games stressing skills in accordance with the children's abilities and growth in vocabulary skills.

The concept of coats being needed for winter may be extended to broader activities, such as learning the names of some of the fabrics and materials from which coats and other clothing are made. The children should have the opportunity to see and feel some of the materials as they learn the new verbal concepts to describe them. Trips to stores and filmstrips or films may be correlated with these activities.

The understanding of how animals also have warm coats for winter can be more fully acquired through a trip to a farm to:

    a. See some of the animals and learn about their coats, touch them and see how their coats help them in cold weather.

    b. Extend their conceptual growth.

F. *Vocabulary:*

1. Dog, cat, horse, cow, sheep, chicken, rooster, hen, turkey, lamb, pony, kittens, puppies, fur, sleek, shiny, rough, various colors of animals' fur, feathers, beak, bill, bark, mew, neigh, whinny, bleat, crow, cackle, gobble, run, scamper, gallop, trot, strut, scratch, etc.

G. *Supplementary Activities:*

1. Slides or photographs may be taken of the animals and trip experiences. As they are shown in the classroom, the children may answer questions about them or use them in language development games.

This outline has been presented as a sample of the many possibilities for vocabulary development through self-care skills and extended experiences. Similar experiences may be involved in the teaching of other personal care skills.

II. *Learning to Recognize Fruits and Vegetables*

This activity may be first introduced through the use of bright colorful pictures of fruits and vegetables. The teacher may tell the children the names of them, and they may talk about their colors, those that contain leaves, and their other obvious characteristics.

The class may then plan a trip to a supermarket to see the vegetables, and experiences that involve preparation of fruits and vegetables may be planned.

A. *Activities:*
  1. Preparing fruits for Jell-O®.
  2. Preparing vegetables for a tossed salad.
  3. Making vegetable soup.
  4. Making applesauce.
  5. Cooking cranberries for sauce.

  Much supportive help and supervision by the teacher will be needed for these activities, but they offer possibilities for vocabulary growth, safety and health instruction. Many of the disadvantaged children have not had sufficient home instruction in these activities. They may not have had the experience of helping their mothers make cookies, etc. They need the help necessary for learning to use the stove carefully, cleanliness in food preparation, and tidiness in work. The children need guidance and help to learn good judgment in regard to kinds of foods that are best for each meal, how to shop, and other homemaking skills.

B. *Vocabulary:* (Possible new concepts)
  1. Grapes, apples, bananas, nuts, fruit cocktail, Jell-O, sugar, stir, boiling water, dissolve, lettuce, carrots, radishes, tomatoes, onions, salt, salad dressing, vinegar and oil, thousand island dressing, French dressing and others, applesauce, cinnamon, spices, soup, broth, seasoning, potatoes, beef or soup bone, celery, and others.

  The children should have many experiences involving the preparing, eating and learning the names of fruits and vegetables. Plastic or other miniature fruits and vegetables may be used in a variety of ways as review activities.

C. *Supplementary Activities* may also include:
  1. The use of the opaque projector for the presentation of pictures. The children may be asked to indicate fruits and vegetables that the teacher names, or they may name

them and call upon another student to indicate the named ones.

2. Charts may be prepared with bright colorful pictures. Corresponding sets of smaller cards may contain individual pictures. The teacher may hold up a card, saying, "This card has the picture of a potato on it. Find another potato like it on the big chart."

3. Vegetable and fruit "Match Game" cards may be prepared with pictures for all of the squared sections. The pictures may be of fruits or vegetables, and a good representation of the categories may be contained on each card. The teacher may have a "master" set of fruit and vegetable picture cards. These may be small index cards each containing a picture. The teacher may hold up the picture cards individually and name the picture. The children will cover their squares each time that their cards contain the specified fruit or vegetable picture. The first child to have his card covered wins the game and may be "It," and hold up the cards for the next game. The other children should be encouraged to help in naming the pictures if the leader needs this help. The purpose of the game is to strive to learn the names of the fruits and vegetables as well as to share and help each other.

4. Seatwork tasks may involve drawing lines from bright pictures of fruits and vegetables from one side of the paper to corresponding ones on the other side. Later seatwork activities may involve plain outlined pictures or stenciled ones.

5. The children may learn to color fruits and vegetables correctly by looking at a display of real ones in the room. Plastic or wax miniatures may be used, also.

6. Scrapbook preparation may involve pictures cut from magazines. Fruits and vegetables may be classified through organization and their pictures pasted on certain pages.

Other areas providing possibilities for vocabulary

building experiences may include housekeeping skills, such as table setting.

Doll house furniture is helpful in learning the names of furniture and the rooms in which it belongs. The children may be helped in preparing a section of the floor by using masking tape outlined "rooms." They may place the model furniture in the correct room of their "house." A room may be similarly "furnished" in a shoe box or carton with small plastic furniture.

Flat pictures of furniture may be arranged into the right "room" on a flannel board "house" which is sectioned by yarn or narrow felt strips. Labels, such as "Kitchen," "Living Room," etc. may be placed above each sectioned room.

Many other language developmental activities may be correlated with these experiences.

Vocabulary

The need to start early in the child's life to develop his vocabulary and provide the needed experiential and conceptual background has been emphasized by many who are exploring the needs of the disadvantaged child and organizing the Head Start programs. Lloyd lists this as one of the important avenues of attack in meeting the reading needs.

> All-out efforts will be made in the years ahead to *encourage earlier language development* and to build necessary concepts. We know that language patterns are firmly implanted by the time a child is six years old. Therefore, the socially disadvantaged child must have our help with language and concept development in the preschool years.[52]

The children need help through the use of real objects to understand abstract concepts, such as those that tell size, position, or are used to make comparisons. This help must be given through direct experiences with the use of materials as well as many oppor-

---

[52]From Helene M. Lloyd: What's ahead in reading for the disadvantaged? *The Reading Teacher*, March, 1965, Vol. 18, No. 6, pp. 471-2. Courtesy of International Reading Association.

tunities to use and hear the vocabulary words to express the meanings. Some suggested activities to help are listed below.

The Concept of Big and Little

A variety of pairs of objects which the children are readily able to name may be shown in pairs including a big and little one of each. "This is the *big* ball. Here is the *little* ball." (Big and little books, dolls, toy trucks, cars, etc., may also be used.)

The children then may take turns coming up to the table and pointing to the big or little object that the teacher has named or requested. The student then may name an object, ask for a big or little one and choose someone to find it.

The relative meaning of big and little (this ball is big in comparison with this one, but it is little when it is compared with a larger one) should not be introduced until the children have mastered the sequential beginning steps in the comparison skill. Teaching aims for these activities are related to the vocabulary development and understanding at first, and so the thinking and decision-making skills should be introduced only as the child is ready. Activities involving basic and clearly defined skills which are few in number should be introduced in the beginning with much reinforcement and presentation of new skills and concepts as the learner is ready to receive this instruction.

The Concept of Tall and Short

This may be introduced through having some of the older boys and girls from other rooms to come in and help if possible. The teacher may have a tall and short child stand up. Explanatory sentences could describe the meaning of the concept.

"Fred is tall. Bill is short. Look, Bill's head comes up only to Fred's shoulders. Fred is this much taller." (Indicate by placing one hand on Bill's head and hold the other one up even with the top of Fred's.)

Different pairs of students may stand up to show who is tall and who is short. The others may be asked to tell the names of the children and whether they are tall or short.

The comparative meaning of tall and short should not be introduced until the children are ready to benefit from this instruction. (Bill is tall now, because Joe is the shorter boy, etc.)

Comparison of sizes involving three children may be presented as the children are ready for this concept. "Who is tallest?"

Pictures of tall and short people may be collected from magazines and backed with flannel for use on the flannel or felt board for reinforcement activities.

The Concept of Here and There

This may be introduced through experiences to help the child realize that *here* or *there* depends upon an object's location in relation to oneself.

The teacher may introduce the concept through a series of explanatory activities, such as the ones below.

"This chair is *here*. I am standing by it, and so it is near me. This red chair is here. The other blue chair is over there in the corner. The blue chair is *there*. It is not by me. It is *there*." (Indicate other things that are *here* and those that are *there*.)

The purpose for this introduction is to add these words, *here* and *there,* to the learner's vocabulary of understood meanings or conceptual understanding, and so effort should be used to provide opportunities for use of these new words in sentences. The children may take turns using these words in simple requests, questions or answers to each other's questions, such as:

"Bring that blue book *here* to me."

"Take this chair over *there* to the window."

Some children may be directed to stand by certain objects or have them on their desks. Other students may ask such questions as, "Where is the eraser?"

Another child may answer, "It is *here* on my desk," or "It is *there* on the table."

A game may be played in which a group of objects are placed in various positions around the room. Children who are "It" may be directed to stand in a certain place. Another child may name an object, and the child who is "It" tells the answer by indicating whether it is *here* or *there* in relation to its proximity to himself.

Another activity may include the direction for the child to go anyplace in the room or by any child's seat. He may ask, "Where am I, Bill?" Bill may say, "You are *there*." (Or *here,* according to how close the child is to himself.)

The children should each have a turn to refer to themselves as *here* or *there* in relation to their positions and that of their classmates. Objects may be used to vary the activity but also reinforce the same two concepts and provide for supplementary use of language skills.

The students may be encouraged to talk about things outdoors as being out *there;* things indoors as in *here.*

"Where is a big tree? Is it in *here* or out *there?*"

"Is the piano in *here* or out *there?*"

Other concepts that should be introduced through explanatory-experiences are the following.

Up and Down

Putting objects on high and low shelves and saying, "This book is *up* on this shelf." "The top is *down* on this shelf."

Holding things up and down and saying, "I am holding the ball *up* high."

"Now, I am putting the ball *down* on the floor."

Giving directions to each other to put a certain object up or down.

Putting felt objects up or down in position on the flannel board.

Conversation that involves description of the positions or indicates whether the objects are up or down should accompany these activities. This conversation should be done by both teacher and pupils.

Under and Over

This may be introduced through a gym activity in which the children throw a volley ball over or under the net. Conversation used by the teacher and students to give directions may be as this: "Eddie, throw the ball *over* the net," etc.

Top and Bottom

Shelves, lockers, bookcases, etc. may be used for putting toys on the *top* shelves, books on the bottom, etc. The group discussion that goes on during these activities may be especially helpful for language development and understanding of new concepts.

Near and Far

This may be introduced by talking about how the things in the room are *near,* but what is seen outdoors is *far* away.

Trips, such as to the airport may be utilized to reinforce these concepts. Planes that have landed at the airport and are near the children and those that are leaving or are far away should be observed and discussed in sentences that describe the conceptual meanings.

Walks around the school area to observe houses that are near and those that are far away can help to strengthen the pupil understanding of these concepts.

The unique aspect of instruction for the disadvantaged child lies not only in how it is presented, but in the fact that it must not be assumed that the learner has necessarily already mastered a concept. Instruction must provide for diagnosis of pupil needs and evaluation of growth as well as the presentation of new content. It is important to start where the children are in each area, and such appraisal of pupil needs is continuous, and as each pupil lack of understanding of a conceptual meaning is revealed, the lesson should then be directed toward the aim of providing for this need.

Examples of teacher provision for newly revealed pupil misconceptions of word meanings are the ways in which Mrs. Alta Ford at Preston School and Mrs. Arthur W. Farrell, Courville School in Detroit, Michigan provide the needed materials when necessary to help the children gain new experiences. When the teacher was talking about dandelions during a lesson and found that her students visualized a dandelion as some grandiose animal, she stopped the planned lesson and the class went out to pick dandelions.

During another class activity the teacher asked the pupils if they knew from what source feathers come. Many hands were raised. One child said, "Yes, we all know where feathers come from. They come from pillows." A farm visit to see and touch chickens, ducks and other poultry helped to clarify this misunderstanding.

When Mrs. Ford's class visited a dairy, a child who was observing the milk dispensing machine as it filled the rotating bottles with milk, asked her teacher, "It that the cow?"

A continuous awareness by the teacher of the concepts that are new to the children demands, as the needs becomes apparent, for time and effort to clarify these meanings for the children. If a story contains a word that any one or many pupils do not understand, it must be explained and the needed experience provided.

Picture recognition can be helpful in building the child's vocabulary if it is supplemented by needed real experiences for each concept. Pictures of fruit or vegetables that are new to the pupils should be supplemented with experiences in which they eat, handle, name the color, and make comparisons with the help of the teacher. Animals on the farm or in the zoo must be seen as well as observed in picture books.

Filmstrips that contain many pictures may be used for picture recognition. The children may find and indicate the pictures named by the teacher, and repeat their verbal symbols. They may take turns naming pictured objects and calling upon their classmates to find them when a sufficient recognition background is developed. More filmstrips to aid in concept development are needed. Most of the picture filmstrips now available are those prepared for other instructional purposes, such as the development of ability to distinguish initial consonant sounds, rhyming words, etc. These are helpful, and they can be adapted to other teaching aims, too, but more of this type of instructional media are needed.

The concept of likenesses and differences should be introduced first by the use of very simple objects, shapes or designs. They must be very easy to be distinguished in their likenesses or differences as compared with others. This concept should be first introduced by use of gross objects, such as the following.

1. Two red balls and a blue truck. The teacher may talk to the children about how the two balls are the same, but the truck is different.
2. Hold up a red ball. Ask the child to point to another ball on the table. Explain that the two balls are the same, and mention various similarities, such as they are both round, red, and are played with in games or for bouncing, etc.

3. Ask a child to choose the toy that has wheels, one that bounces or those that fit other such similar descriptions. If the child cannot find the one that bounces from that description, pick up the ball and bounce it, saying, "The ball bounces like this."

4. A felt board may be arranged with four snap clothes pins fastened to ribbons, or bias mending tape. The tape or ribbon may be fastened to the top of the board with metal clamps. This device provides for the use of small three dimensional objects, such as plastic or wooden blocks, toy airplanes, cars, etc.

a. The concept of differences may be introduced or reinforced through the use of this "Clip Board Device." Three plastic blocks and one toy truck may be hooked in a row to the ribbons or tape, as they are gripped by the clothespins. The children may be asked to point to all of the blocks, find the toy truck, etc. This activity may be varied through the variety of small inexpensive objects that are available. (Fig. 35). This is described more fully in Chapter XII.

b. After the children have had much practice in indicating the described objects, the use of the words, "Which one is different?" or "Which ones are all alike?" may be used and supplemented with needed help and explanations.

c. Children and parents may help the teacher to collect many interesting little objects for use on the "Clip Board." Anything from small toys, prizes from Cracker Jacks, to small ornaments or decorations may be collected. Very small items may be prepared for better visibility by having a strip of Scotch tape doubled and placed on the back to be hooked into the clothespins.

5. Flat objects or pictures that are simple in detail may be used with the flannel board.

6. Objects may be placed on the child's desk or the table for the class to take turns indicating those that are alike or different.

The skill of simple classifying should not be introduced until the children have acquired a sufficient experiential background in object recognition, understanding of concepts, and distinguishing likenesses and differences. They need sufficient verbal ability to describe and generalize their observations. When the objects are

Figure 35. Clip board device for concrete objects.

presented to the children for classification, they should first be few in number and very familiar through previous experiences concerning them. Beginning classification activities may be done through the following:

1. From a group of airplanes and cars, the children may be told to put all of the airplanes in one box; the cars in another.

2. After many experiences with the flannel board and concrete objects to be classified, the children may make simple classifications of pictures. They may separate pictures of things to eat from those for play. These pictured objects may be pasted in scrapbooks or they may be pasted individually on small cards to be classified and placed in groups by the children. This pro-

vides for the classification activity to be done many times with the use of the same picture collection. The cards may include new groupings added later as the children are ready to classify objects according to several categories.

3. Classification activities involving independent pasting of pictures by the child should be introduced as he is ready and has mastered the skills involved. An example of this is a seatwork sheet with toys at the bottom, and the top of the paper is divided into two sectioned sides labeled "Boys" and "Girls." The child is directed to cut out the toys and paste those for a boy and girl in their proper sections on the paper.

4. Classification of shapes, forms, and more abstract items may be introduced by having the child place construction paper shapes in small boxes or cartons. This should first require that the child choose only from two items, such as two colors, two shapes, etc. Such directions may be given as follows:

> "Put the red circles in this box; put the blue ones in this box like this." Working with the child until he is well started or clearly understands may be necessary.

> Later the children may classify squares, circles, etc. by placing them in the designated boxes.

> Classifying several shapes, colors, or objects may be done later. Finer classification should be introduced only as the children are ready for this skill.

5. Audiovisual aids that may also be used in classification are filmstrips, the overhead and opaque projectors.

6. Walks may be utilized for the purpose of observing certain specified things and indicating them. The children may be directed to find all they can of certain kinds of buildings, plants, people who do different kinds of work, vehicles, etc. This activity involves many things that have been seen before by the pupils, but a new skill can be reinforced through the clearly defined purposes involved in this class walk.

The Meaning of First, Last, and Middle

They are introduced in the above order, because it seems easier for the children to learn the meaning of "first" and "last" before "middle" is introduced.

The teacher may place three large construction paper circles on the board, saying, "This one is first, this one is last, but this one is in the middle." The children may be called upon to take turns standing by the first, last or middle circles. When three children are standing to represent each circle and its position, the teacher may say, "The first child sit down," etc. Each time a child sits down, he may be instructed to call upon a classmate to take his place, saying, "Joe, come up and be first" (or last, in the middle, etc.).

Pictures may be placed on the board in the three positions. The children may take turns indicating the position of a picture.

Children may line up in single file order of first, middle and last and march around the room as music is played. When the music stops, everyone must stand still in the line waiting for the direction, such as, "The first child sit down" (or the middle, etc.). "Billy, you are the first child. Choose someone else to be first." "When the music stops the next time, the last child must sit down and choose someone else to be last."

Later, after more help is provided in which the meanings are presented through other additional activities thus permitting needed reinforcement, the children will be able to transfer their understanding to enable them to find "first," "last," etc. in a row of pictures in books or other settings. They may use the words in games. The children should be given as many opportunities as possible to use their new concepts verbally in meaningful situations.

Readiness Seatwork Activities. These possibly may serve a special need of the disadvantaged child. Very interesting seatwork can be helpful to these children who need to grow in independence and ability to complete a task by themselves. This may include cutting and pasting, coloring, indicating certain pictures or other items by drawing lines under, marking with an X or circling.

Some independent activities may be the permanent type that may be used many times. Examples of this are matching objects that are alike, sorting tasks, and puzzles, etc. Small boxes or cartons may be used to prepare a variety of interesting independent tasks. The children need activities that involve handling, examining and using concrete objects. This is especially so during the pre-reading stages when the children are learning to work independently for the first time and need to feel confident about their abilities.

Activities that the children can do in small groups are also needed for the disadvantaged children. They also must have opportunities to choose the tasks that they may wish to do and to decide whether they prefer to work alone or with other children. The lives of these children include few choices outside of their school experiences, and so they need to learn to choose and to enjoy the privilege of choosing as well as learning to follow directions.

These children need many experiences that provide auditory discrimination skills, sensory training, ability to form mental and sensory images, and ability to do cognitive thinking.

There is a great need for much classroom action research to evaluate instructional techniques and educational learning aids as well as to determine pupil needs. Follow-up and case studies to determine pupil success resulting from educational measures to educate the disadvantaged child are needed.

The purpose of this chapter has not been to attempt to cover all or even very many of the readiness skills with which the disadvantaged child needs special attention, but to possibly present a few instructional techniques that may help to provide for the need. There is a great need for teacher sharing of techniques and materials, and all educators who are concerned with helping this child must strive to present workable basic techniques that may be applied in the effort to realize definite instructional aims as defined by pupil needs.

Even one new idea that is helpful in any way to meet the needs of the children is a great contribution.*

---

*The presentation of "First," "Last" and "Middle" is reprinted from "Language Development for the Trainable" by Mary Lou Durbin, *The Pointer for Special Class Teachers and Parents of the Handicapped* (Vol. II, No. 2, 1966 pp. 45-6. The Association for Special Class Teachers and Parents of the Handicapped, Inc.).

Chapter XI

AUDIOVISUAL AIDS IN READING READINESS

THE CONSTANT EXPOSURE of the child to television including its increasing number of verbal symbols, the possible broadened scope of learning afforded by this viewing, and the contributions of science and space explorations to the lives and knowledge of children present a greater than ever challenge for teachers to creatively utilize audiovisual aids and their direct instructional techniques in meeting pupil needs.

The child's leisure time is often monopolized by the TV screen's offering of entertainment through viewing and listening. Books, radio, and especially television have been referred to as the "phantom curriculum."[53] The school cannot ignore its responsibilities in the effort to bridge the span between what may be merely the representations of abstract things caused by the child's passive observing and listening and his realization of real experiences as being pertinent to his life. Much guidance from the teacher is needed to prevent this large portion of the child's time from being used in an aimless or unconstructive manner. The extent of the child's whole life curriculum must be realized and considered; what he reads or views on television at home, what opportunities he may have to travel, observe, do, listen and otherwise participate in, and how these activities add enrichment to his life experiences. The opportunities with which a child has been privileged to become more aware of the beautiful sights to experience and enjoy in his world are very significant. The lack of magazines or picture books, music and art appreciation to motivate and facilitate learning in the homes of some children, must be realized and the necessary provision caused through the school program.

---

[53]From Harold G. Shane, June Mulry, Mary E. Reddin, and Margaret C. Gillespie, *loc. cit.* pp. 11-12.

Edgar Dale summarized direct and indirect experiences and the concrete and abstract in a "Cone of Experience." The base of Dale's Cone represents direct reality itself as we experience it first hand.

> It is the rich, full-bodied experience that is the bed rock of all education. It is the purposeful experience that is seen, handled, tasted, touched, felt, and smelled. It is the unabridged version of life itself.[54]

The rest of Dale's Cone includes his summary of the experiences from the direct to the indirect according to their placement on the Cone.

> The cone is not offered as a perfect or mechanically flawless picture to be taken with absolute literalness in its simplified form. *It is merely a visual aid* in explaining the interrelationships of the various types of audiovisual materials, as well as their individual "positions" in the learning process.[55]

Direct, purposeful experiences are the real basis for all education, but they have a special importance and significance to growth in reading readiness and later skills. Reading is such a complex process requiring mastery of printed symbols and their application to meanings, many of which also embrace several concepts. Each of these printed symbols can be associated by the child only with the meaning that has grown through his own experiences. A backlog of experiences previous to his exposure to the printed words are a "must" to enable the child to bring to the fore what is needed from his background to associate his special meaning to what he sees in the word symbols.

> Reading involves the recognition of printed or written symbols which serve as stimuli for the recall of meanings built up through the reader's past experience. New meanings are derived through manipulation of concepts already in his possession.[56]

---

[54]Dale, Edgar: *Audio-visual Methods in Teaching,* Revised Edition. Copyright 1954, Holt, Rinehart and Winston, Inc.

[55]Dale, Edgar, *Ibid.*

[56]From Guy L. Bond, and Miles A. Tinker, *loc. cit.,* p. 19.

There is apparently the need for an even greater balanced use of the various audiovisual aids in teaching that includes greater emphasis upon the direct and concrete and more directed interpretation of the indirect and abstract. This instruction as presented through the use of audiovisual aids may cause the abstract concepts to become more clearly realized by the learner.

The final stage or pinnacle of Dale's Cone is devoted to verbal symbols. Verbal symbols are as far from direct, purposeful experiences as the distance between the North and South Poles if these symbols are forced to shift for themselves without the supportive help of other accompanying aids or techniques to clarify their intended meaning. Children are, however, too often exposed to verbal symbols alone without sufficient experiences or other aids to permit full understanding of ideas. This is especially detrimental to the learning of the slower students who need much repetition, reinforcement and supplementary help to provide review of the same skills formerly introduced but not fully grasped by the learner. Many students who have not mastered the readiness skills should have the benefit of a variety of audiovisual aids used as tools to reintroduce the same skills through a new interest-creating medium.

Dale stresses the need and the fact that these verbal symbols can be made meaningful to every child.

> Thus the pinnacle of the cone is not a rarified height frequented only by the great intellects. It is the common ground for every human being who can talk and listen.[57]

Although verbal symbols are aids in themselves, they need the help of other audiovisual aids. Dependence upon verbal symbols with very little or no help from the other media causes pupil inattention, lack of interest and inability to grasp the concept or learning skill.

> Verbal symbols, therefore, are used together with every other material on the cone, though they themselves are abstractions.[58]

The application of more audiovisual aids is needed in planning for the developmental sequence of skills, and provision is necessary

---

[57]Dale, Edgar, *loc. cit.*, p. 53.
[50]Dale, Edgar, *Ibid.*, p. 53.

for their use as supplementary aids to reinforcement at any skill level needed by the learner. An interesting variety of activities to provide for time and sufficient practice until the pupil masters the skills will also permit the student to explore, develop worthwhile attitudes and interests as well as to grow intellectually and emotionally through the learning experience.

Audiovisual aids offer many opportunities to meet the slower student's need for repetition and the bright or gifted student's demands for enrichment through supplementary activities and possibilities for his creative growth and expression.

The present abundant availability of instructional materials and devices necessitates the instructor's discernment and wise application of audiovisual aids to the techniques applied and their expected learning outcomes. The need to more specifically and purposefully evaluate these aids and to carefully apply them where their possibilities can be realized and their limitations supplemented by the use of others can be fulfilled through the constant effort to understand pupil needs and plan curriculum goals accordingly. Teacher insight into pupil needs, creativity in planning and devising instructional techniques and devices as well as the ability to choose valuable instructional aids from the available sources are even more necessary because of the broad scope provided by the materials and various media.

The Need for Teacher-planned Learning Aids

More visual aid materials or suggestions for teacher prepared devices to effect learning at the developmental levels, thus enabling provision to be permitted for certain growth stages, are needed as well as the type of aids that can be used for testing and diagnosis of weaknesses. Many visual-aid materials progress rapidly from the very easy to the difficult without sufficient sequence of skills. They often include the use of merely a few items or pages. Perhaps if the school systems, through teacher representative committees, and the commercial firms could work even more closely together in the planning and interpretation of pupil needs and the preparation of materials to provide for this developmental skill aspect of learning, more sequence of skills could possibly be considered in the designs of learning aids. Although many consultants for the firms have a background in education, more enlistment of in-service teachers is needed. Through their daily contact with existing pupil needs, they are aware of possibilities for effectively designed commercial materials to provide for specific learning handicaps and the necessary sequential aspect of instruction. More is being done in this way than has been in the past but much more is needed to keep abreast of the growing need.

There are many supplementary workbooks available in the stores or supermarkets. Although much can be done by parents to supplement their child's school activities, the use of this supplementary material to teach skills should best be done with the guidance of the teacher. Homework that is most effective is the type that reinforces skills already introduced in class or involves pupil reading or research for reports and special assignments. Parents wishing to give their child additional help should be sure that the methods involved are the same as those through which their child has been introduced to a skill at school, or at least that they are not contrary to school instruction. These workbooks that cover a variety of subjects and are very inexpensive, have much to offer, but those that involve the presentation of skills should be used according to the recommendations of the child's teacher. Some of these workbooks have been most effective when used by a child's tutor or in summer school remedial classes, also.

Contributions of Filmstrips

Some filmstrips for teaching likenesses and differences contain many skills including scrutiny for varied details, as found in shape, size, position and minute internal details. The greatest pupil benefit can be derived from these filmstrips if they are used following the teaching of visual discrimination skills in step-by-step sequences and with the application of a variety of instructional aids and techniques. After the testing and review of skills through the use of filmstrips, reteaching or reinforcement through practice at the skill levels where the need is indicated by pupil performance should supplement the filmstrip and previous instruction.

More help could be made available through the use of such

filmstrips if they were prepared to follow the sequence of skills in the areas emphasized. Although many are designed to stress similarities or differences, their emphasis ranges from simple outlined shapes to extremely fine internal or varied detail in pictured objects and other types of discrimination all in one filmstrip. Although the filmstrip may be an expensive type of visual aid for individual teachers to assume the responsibility for preparation, perhaps more teacher participation in the designing or planning of them would be helpful. This planning could be done through teacher committees, and recommendations offered according to the outcome of this group effort. Filmstrip firms would perhaps welcome this type of suggestion concerning future needs to be met through the preparation of their product. More series of filmstrips with each strip emphasizing one skill area and others that are designed for testing purposes and review are needed.

School Grade Level Committees

Grade level committees in some school systems include all teachers concerned with each grade level or subject area. Special institutes are held periodically throughout the school year during which these teachers meet according to their respective grade or subject levels. The purpose is to center the planning of topics and secure speakers according to the suggestions and recommendations of the group. Outcomes of this staff effort are included in each grade level report to the administrative council to make possible each teacher's opportunity to participate in the steering of the curriculum planning through this representation of the faculty groups. It seems that these faculty groups could possibly contribute much more relative to evaluations of and suggestions for commercially prepared materials for use within their grade levels and subject areas. The preparation of audiovisual aids to involve sequential skill development and additional repetition at needed levels is a problem area worthy of such consideration.

Help Offered by the Coordinator

More sharing of audiovisual materials, especially the teacher prepared ones that have proven successful could be possible through the guidance of the building audiovisual coordinator.

Such sharing would facilitate the use of a variety of materials, and avoid unnecessary expense due to duplication that is caused when each teacher must prepare most of the materials needed for one's own class. Teachers of kindergarten or other pre-reading students may share ideas, sources and materials within their buildings and may continually be aware of new materials and techniques through the guidance of the audiovisual coordinator and committee.

More effort should be directed to the devising of instructional aims, realization of pupil needs and more purposefully applying techniques and learning aids. Teachers must not only be continually aware of what learning aids are available, but must also define needs and offer suggestions for the provision of needed materials.

The tremendous and ever growing supply of commercially prepared materials does not in any way minimize the need for teacher prepared and devised instructional aids. Teacher effort to devise or create avenues to helping a pupil grasp a concept or learn a skill ranks "tops" in the goals of an audiovisual aids program. It also is instrumental in inspiring student creativity. Activities that involve the use of scrap materials or something that the child may have available at home or otherwise obtain through his own efforts are often more intriguing, attention-capturing and interest-sustaining than that which may be easily purchased. The teacher must be cognizant of the possible scope of the audio-visual aids program and its opportunities to utilize a variety of devices for needed repetition, reinforcement of learning skills, and supplementary activities. The overuse of one or two media can defeat learning purposes through the loss of pupil interest, yet the attention span can be renewed to permit additional help for the same skill with the use of a different instructional aid.

School Audiovisual Services

Much can be done through the school or system-wide audiovisual program such as the one in Garden City, Michigan. This program is under the leadership of the audiovisual director whose responsibilities may include the ordering of films, filmstrips, A-V equipment and other materials to be purchased by the school or borrowed from the county audiovisual center, guiding the steering committee representing all schools throughout the system, and serving as teacher consultant. A committee of building coordinators who represent their respective schools within the system are responsible to and under the leadership of the director. Planning and leadership of the A-V director and the representative committee of coordinators provides opportunities for the teachers to request materials in advance for the following year or for their immediate use and make suggestions for the purchase of new equipment.

The building A-V coordinators are responsible for representing their building co-workers in the program, the care and use of equipment in their building and serving as teacher consultants. It is highly recommended that each teacher who may not have previously mastered the operation of all audiovisual equipment should seek help in learning to do so. Much more can be accomplished through the application of this equipment to pupil and class needs if the teacher can readily operate the equipment. Student pride in their teacher's competence concerning control of these impressive and interesting machines and the self-confidence of the teacher who can set up a sound projector, utilize the films in class activities, re-wind or splice films, are far from unimportant reasons to be considered. It seems worthwhile for teachers to strive to earn the pride of their students. The convenience of each teacher's ability to use the equipment whenever it may serve an instructional need for the particular class is, however, the most important reason for every individual teacher to learn to operate the equipment. This also permits experimentation with the equipment and ample opportunities to devise new ways in which it can be used. The A-V building coordinator may conduct workshops within the building during which all teachers who wish may have help with the operation of equipment. The sharing of ideas is possible through these workshops, also.

The description that will follow in the next chapter concerns the various ways that audio-visual aids may be used in the introduction of the readiness skills and will emphasize the skills as well as the audiovisual aids because of the versatility of the instructional devices and techniques. The possible application of many devices to stress one skill and the ways that the same instructional devices may be applied to various skills in several ways will be shown throughout the described activities.

The role of audiovisual aids in the readiness program is very important concerning the needs of the child who is delayed in such skills. The child can profit from a prolonged, varied and intensely interesting program of activities before he is introduced to formal reading instruction. Audiovisual aids may help to make this additional help possible. Readiness skills, the audiovisual media, and the activities, techniques and ways of application for sequential skill development will be described. The purpose is not to describe all of the readiness skills or all of the possibilities for instruction through audiovisual materials, but to tell how some skills can be introduced in sequential development, reinforcement, reteaching and possibilities for supplementary practice to be given through this program.

Chapter XII

READINESS SKILLS AND AUDIOVISUAL MEDIA

Vocabulary and Recognition of Objects

Media

Real life experiences, objects, picture books, flannel board, Hook N' Loop Board, films and filmstrips and projection transparencies to be used with the opaque or overhead projectors.

Actual experiences, such as trips to the farm, zoo, dairy and others permit the child to see, hear, touch, fully appreciate, and really become more aware of all that is involved in his new experiences. The ability to remember the names of new animals, objects and sounds through this first-hand experience is more easily acquired. Nothing can contribute more to a child's readiness background than these real life experiences. These have been placed at the very base of Dale's Cone. When the child later reads about farm animals, he will form mental images of how they sound, what they eat, and how soft their fur feels to his touch.

A variety of experiences for increasing the child's conceptual vocabulary may include stories read by the teacher or parent and activities involving learning the names of concrete objects, miniature ones or those prepared from other materials. Naming or indicating these things in recognition games will be enjoyed by the child.

The pre-readers need many opportunities to name objects, talk about them, and make associations or otherwise recall the verbal symbol that denotes each one.

Catalogs, stamp premium books and other available sources for pictured objects may be utilized. If a child merely names the pictures on each page, answers questions about them, tells what they may be used with, and describes them, this experience helps him to

189

gain confidence in his verbal ability, and provides readiness for later skill in noting details in reading, telling in order the events of a story and summarizing the action.

The opaque and overhead projectors may be used for the child to name the pictured objects. Any picture can be presented, plain or in color from a magazine or workbook through the use of the opaque projector. Projection transparencies can be used with the overhead projector as well as the opaque. The flannel board felt objects may be placed on the overhead projector and they can be projected in shadow or opaque form on the chalkboard or screen. The children may be asked to indicate them as they are named. They may do this by pointing with a yardstick or long pointer. The students may be asked to name the pictures, in rows to provide for left-to-right progression skill, tell what is *above* or *below* certain pictures, tell how some may be used, whether or not they make noise, which are big or little, and give many other descriptions in a variety of activities.

Filmstrips that are available for rhyming and phonetic skills can also be used in the readiness program to aid in picture recognition, left-to-right progression and the other skills named above. These filmstrips contain pictures that are prepared for the presentation of rhyming objects to be named, but they can also be used in the development of picture recognition and vocabulary skills.

Left-to-right Progression Skills

Media

Pictures, opaque and overhead projectors. The flannel board and felt objects may be used with the overhead projector for left-to-right progression skills. The children may trace around them being directed to always begin at a designated place at the left and working to the right. This tracing may be done if the figures are projected onto a newsprint or shelfpaper "screen." An easel may be used to support the paper "screen" as the child works.

Colorful or plain pictures may be glued in rows on construction paper or on tagboard cards. They can be projected onto a screen through the use of the opaque projector. Transparencies containing pictures in rows may also be prepared for use with the overhead projector. The child may name the pictures from left to right. If several rows are prepared, they will afford the opportunity for the child to practice the left to right and return sweep skill necessary for reading. Learning to follow rows in order and with ease when naming pictures provides some readiness experience preparatory to learning to follow rows or words.

Gross Visual Discrimination of Likenesses and Differences
Media

Flannelboard and felt objects, Hook N' Loop Board, pegboard, a great variety of three dimensional objects, overhead and opaque projectors, and a hand-made tachistoscopic device to be described.

Ability To See Differences

It seems to be easier for the child to grasp the concept of "Which one is different?" first. Then the meaning of likenesses may more easily be presented following mastery of the former skill.

Felt and Flannel Board Drills. Three felt figures of the same color and one object different in both shape and color may be placed in a row on the flannel board. *Example*: Three red apples and one green pear. The child indicates the "different" one.

Next may come three felt figures of the same color and one that is different in shape but the same as the others in color. *Example:* Three yellow chickens and one yellow square.

Four objects which are the same in both shape and color, but one is in a grossly different position may be presented next. *Example:* Four green pears, three standing erect, but one lying sideways.

Four objects which are alike in shape and color, but one is in a finer different position may follow. *Example:* Four orange circles with one placed slightly above the others in the line.

Four objects which are alike in shape and color may include one placed in a reversed position in the line. *Example:* Four yellow chickens, one facing in an opposite direction from the rest.

Differences in internal and varied detail can be emphasized by adding finer details on one figure in the row. A leg, stem or other portion of one figure may be folded under and a detail of this one figure changed to be noted by the child as causing the object to be "different."

Picture cards, those from magazine, catalogs and inexpensive picture books can be prepared for use with the flannel board by gluing a scrap of felt or flannel to the back. Scraps of flannel or felt may be saved for a variety of uses with the flannel board and pictures.

Construction paper figures arranged on a white background may be used involving the same types of figures that have been used with the flannel board. They could be glued to the construction paper background and the child may indicate the difference in each row. This may be done at whatever level of difficulty the children need added reinforcement of learning.

The Hook N' Loop Board may be used for three-dimensional objects, such as colored plastic or wooden alphabet blocks, plastic spoons, toy cars, airplanes, buttons, mosaic tiles, colored pipe cleaners, colored doll clothespins, etc. Three objects that are alike and one different may be used.

The overhead projector may be used with the felt figures.

The pegboard may be arranged with peg placings in rows for the child to indicate differences in color and position.[59] *Examples:* Three green pegs; one yellow. Three pegs in a straight row; one above or below the other (Fig. 36).

The children may be asked to tell whether the difference is at the beginning, in the middle or at the end of the row of pegs. This will help to prepare the child or contribute to his readiness for noting initial, medial and final differences in words later in reading.

A hand-made tachistoscopic device which will be described later in more detail, can be prepared from a small plastic ice cream or cottage cheese carton or from cardboard with a view opening. Adding machine paper or other rolls of paper may be used for the preparation of a "movie" in which pictures, buttons, mosaic tiles and other small objects may be placed in a row for each "slide" section of the movie. As each slide section comes into the child's view, he may indicate the difference. The lid of the

---

[59]Durbin, Mary Lou: Peg board drills for the trainable. *The Pointer.* For Special Class Teachers and Parents of the Handicapped, Vol. 10, No. 2, Ⓒ. 1966, pp. 55-6. Courtesy of The Association for Special Class Teachers and Parents of the Handicapped, Inc. Grass Valley, California.

Figure 36. Pegboard used for visual discrimination.

plastic carton may be cut so that there is a slit sufficiently large
to permit the "movie" to be pulled through. Hosiery or other
flat boxes may be prepared so that there is an opening on one
side for the movie to be viewed and both ends are open for the
"reel" of paper containing the items to be pulled for viewing.

Ability To See Likenesses

Flannel Board Drills. A felt figure may be placed first in line
on the board. A space or a wide line or felt marker may be placed
between the first figure and the others in the row. The row includes various figures including one or more exactly the same as

the first one. The teacher may point to the first one and ask the child to find the others that are exactly like it.

A figure may be placed at the top of the flannel board and various others may be arranged randomly at the bottom. The teacher may indicate the top one and ask the children to find the similar one. A new one then may be placed at the top that is like another one at the bottom. Another child may have a turn to match the likenesses.

The Hook N' Loop Board could be used for indicating likenesses. A three dimensional object could be first in line or at the top. Various others including one like the "key" object could be arranged on the board and the child may be asked to indicate the likenesses.

The pegboard may be used for indicating likenesses as well as differences.

Suggestions for the use of *opaque and overhead projectors* follow in the skill of indicating likenesses and differences.

The same skills previously introduced through one media may be reintroduced or continued through the use of another.

Three-dimensional objects may be placed on the lens plate of the overhead projector such as buttons, tiles and others that can project in a clear shadow or opaque form that is easy to distinguish. The children may be asked to indicate differences, likenesses, small or large ones or to find those that are described in sentences by the teacher. Learning to listen to the whole sentence may be stressed through detailed descriptions that the child must listen to carefully in order to indicate the correct one. A car, airplane, etc. may be on the "screen." A sentence such as, "Find something that I can ride in if I want to take a trip up up very high in the sky." Children need much of this type of listening to follow directions and to grasp the finer details involved in reading for content or meaning. This listening skill, although it does not involve reading the words, can be introduced in the readiness program. The child cannot be expected to be able to listen for minute details overnight at the time when he is first doing formal reading. Listening skills begin early long before the sight vocabulary is introduced.

It seems also that many of the children who have difficulty

with reading would probably have gained benefit from a more prolonged and varied skill developmental emphasis upon visual discrimination of finer details. Children who cannot readily distinguish likenesses and differences in very fine letters will soon become lost in the complex skill requirements required in seeing and remembering the similarities and likenesses in words, especially when the learner is also confronted with word recognition, meanings, paragraph and story comprehension, and the necessity for using these skills in written assignments.

Likenesses and differences in geometric forms may be presented in the following ways:

1. Large sheets of manilla or construction paper on which simple shapes are outlined with a wide felt marker. Three shapes, two alike, one different may be outlined. The child may be asked to indicate which is different or point out the similar ones.

2. The child may match likenesses of figures and shapes. Large sheets of paper may contain the above described figures, but a figure similar to one in the row may be outlined on a small separate square of paper. As the teacher holds up the small square of paper calling attention to its contained shape, the child may find the figure that is like that one.

3. Felt-board figures which may be used to indicate likenesses and differences in color, shape and similarities and differences in direction may be used by both the teacher and pupils during the class activities.

The above activities may be repeated through the use of the opaque projector or the chalk board as a visual aid. If the opaque projector is used, pupil interest will be greatly increased. The children may take turns operating the projector and directing the arrow to indicate the likenesses and differences; otherwise, they may use a pointer. This impressive, yet easy to operate machine is very intriguing to the pupils and affords much needed repetition of lessons to strengthen previously presented skills. This projector is very inexpensive to utilize and requires very little extra preparation of materials for some uses, and also offers many possibilities for creativity in teaching.

The overhead projector, also very easy to operate, can be used for some of the same activities after the preparation of dry mount transparencies that contain the skill activities or drills. There is much that can be offered through teacher sharing of transparencies and materials prepared for the overhead projector. The sharing of ideas, techniques and materials save each teacher valuable time and provide more interesting and varied materials for skill emphasis.

The flannel board provides the opportunity for creative teaching and application of this visual aid to the needs of the students through specially devised materials for its use. The board can be easily constructed if one is not available in the classroom. A sturdy one can be built with a wooden frame and the center covered securely with flannel or felt. A tripod easel to hold the board can be constructed. Double boards that fold together in the middle can be made. A heavy square of corrugated cardboard covered with flannel will do very well, also.

The flannel board has been used especially with the commercially prepared felt or die-cut figures, but this instructional aid has not yet "come into its own" concerning its potential creative possibilities for teacher devised visual aids and applied techniques.

Some special techniques for teaching with the flannel board are listed below.

1. *The flannel board* may be used as a seatwork device on which the children may match colors, pictures, shapes, etc. Individual flannel boards may be made for the children by covering a desk sized square of cardboard with flannel. The children may make these in an art activity period or their parents may be asked to help with the preparation of their boards.

2. *Classification of pictures* could be done in categories on their flannel boards. Clothing for winter, foods that are good for dessert, and many other groupings of pictures could be prepared. Paper doll kits of which children have become tired and no longer care to play with at home will readily be donated by parents if requested. They may be placed on the flannel boards in such groups as "Clothes for Boys," "Clothes for Girls," etc. The teacher may print the titles for their classification groupings on small index cards or cardboard strips. These labels may be kept together and used over and over again by the children as they need them. A class collection of these titles for classification activities could be

kept, used by the group and added to as needed. This use of the printed words to signify their activities will be helpful in the motivation of reading, building a vocabulary of understandings, and helping the children to become verbally competent. Small three-dimensional objects may be used by the children to place on their boards according to a classified pattern.

Children may work individually or in small groups using their flannel boards. Conversation to promote the ability to express themselves in sentences, share and plan may be evident by such statements as:

"I'll put the toys on my board. You put things for work on yours."

The teacher may place a pattern on the large flannel board during a group activity period and ask the children to duplicate this pattern by making one exactly the same on their boards. The children may have individual turns to place a pattern on the teacher's flannel board and ask the students to describe the pattern. Speaking in complete sentences, asking questions, describing and noting details are some of the additional skills that result from these activities.

"What do I have on my board?"

"You have four ducks on your board."

"What color are they?"

"Three are yellow and one is white."

Felt figures that are simple in design may be used, such as red apples, animals, and boats. Felt scraps may be used for cutting detailed parts to be placed on figures to make them different, such as other colored stems to be placed on apples, beaks for ducks, and eyes for animals. Sets of the felt figures and detailed parts may be kept in individual envelopes for each of the children to use during this activity. Much of this preparation of materials for these activities may be done by the children with some help from the teacher.

Basic story figures, such as a queen, king, castle, dragon and others may be ordered through commercial sources. Complete sets of figures illustrating favorite stories are also available. Imagination and creativity of the children may be inspired through encouragement to add their own original story figures for use in telling and illustrating their own original stories. Such story figures may be drawn on art or construction paper, colored, painted, cut out and backed with flannel.

The flannel board may also be used by pupils to illustrate the meanings of new words in their vocabularies. Pictures to depict word meanings may be prepared for use on the flannel board as the pupils present these new concepts to their classmates. Various meanings for the same word may be illustrated by pictures.

Examples are *close:* Pictures to show how close may mean to shut a door and when the same spelling may be applied but different pronunciation, the word may mean to be near; and *cross.* Pictures to show how it may mean to go across or to be cross or angry.

Word opposites, such as "big" and "little" may be illustrated. The children may draw their pictures for illustrations or cut them from magazines or other sources to show the word meanings.

Incidental learnings motivated by these activities are numerous, but some important ones are listed below.

1. Gaining self-confidence and poise through many opportunities to share ideas and express one's thoughts to the other students.
2. The ability to clearly present one's ideas so that others can understand what is meant. This ability to communicate with others is important in the reading readiness period.
3. Learning to listen and respect the ideas of others as well as one's own. Learning to wait for others to have a turn, when to help and when to permit others to complete a task unaided.
4. Opportunities to use one's imagination and creative ideas in activities that can be shared.
5. Purposeful correlations of other learning areas, such as art with readiness skill learning.

The Hook N' Loop Board is the newest dimension in visual display boards for presenting instructional aims and concepts through concrete objects. This board which can also be used as a flannel board, contains nylon hooked tape with tiny loops that interlock and anchor three dimensional objects. This is a valuable instructional aid for presenting lessons and can be used for bulletin board displays. The address of the firm where the Hook N' Loop Board may be purchased is given in the list of sources in the last chapter.

The teacher may prepare a clip board device by hooking several metal clamps to the top of a flannel board, cork board or square of heavy cardboard. Each clamp contains a strip of bias mending tape or heavy ribbon. Clothespins that open and close may be glued to the ribbons leaving the teeth of the clothespin free to be opened and closed to clamp onto a three dimensional object. Objects such as small wooden or plastic blocks that cannot be enclosed in the clothespin could be prepared with a three or four inch strip of mending tape that has been doubled together so that the sticky side is on the inside. The clothespins could then be clamped onto the strip of tape leaving the object in plain view of the child. This device has been previously illustrated in Figure 35.

This type of teacher-prepared visual aid is very inexpensive and easily prepared. The clothespins and ribbons may be flipped over and left in back of the board when the teacher and class wish to use the flannel board for flat pictures or felt figures.

The delineascope, which can be used with teacher prepared slides, is a projector that offers possibilities for more contributions to the development of several readiness skills.

The slides may be prepared from two 4¼ x 3½ pieces of glass which are taped together to contain a "film" transparency of white cellophane. To prepare the picture or other instructional items, a carbon is used with the cellophane. Typing or picture stenciling is then done on the carbon and penetrates through to the cellophane.

For projection, the cellophane is placed between the two pieces of glass and placed in the delineascope projection lens. Frosted glass may be used for the preparation of slides. This frosted glass need require only one piece of glass and no cellophane. The preparation may be done right onto the frosted glass slide.

Delineascope slides may be prepared for use with the introduction of the following readiness skills:

1. *What's Wrong?* Pictures that have a part missing or depict a wrong situation may be prepared. The children may tell what is wrong and discuss the situation. These slides are easy to

prepare, since simple pictures may be traced from workbooks and a portion left out.

2. *Likenesses and differences.*

3. *What doesn't belong?* A series of pictures, such as three kinds of fruit and one toy which is the inappropriate thing in the series is presented. The children may tell what doesn't belong and discuss the reasons why.

4. *Which go together?* Two pictured items are shown, such as a ball and bat in a row that contains other pictures. The children indicate which two are used together in the series.

There are many other possibilities for readiness instruction involving the use of this new audiovisual medium. Children may prepare slides, too. This is another interesting device that is motivating and contributes to readiness for learning. The delineascope is available through the Todd Audio-Visual Service, Incorporated.

Coordination Activities for Readiness

Learning to Trace. The overhead projector may be used for kinesthetic finger tracing. White shelf paper or newsprint is available free from newspaper offices with only the request that its containing roller be returned. The paper may be placed on the wall for the presentation of the tracing exercises. A series of broken line tracing series may be prepared on the transparencies, and they may be projected onto the newsprint for the child to "trace" with fingers or with the use of a crayon or pencil. Children who watch the individual who is working and await their turns gain much understanding through this individualized instruction in the group, and the interest is easily held for this activity. This is helpful for left-to-right progression skill as well as coordination. Small transparent plastic bags may serve as a very inexpensive material for the preparation of transparencies. Plastic may also be used. The figures to be projected may be outlined with a felt pen.

The children may make various *line or zigzag patterns* of construction paper that may be placed on the projector lens. They may copy the patterns with their fingers in the air, making wide sweeps from left to right, up or down as the pattern is shown on the screen. This is to develop large muscular control for freedom in coloring and penmanship skills. The children also can use their imaginations to create patterns for this activity.

Learning to Color. Learning to stay within the lines, press down heavily, and finish the coloring task are much more interesting to do with the help of the overhead or opaque projectors. Small construction paper circles, squares, triangles and other figures with the centers cut out, thus producing just a thin construction paper outline, may be placed on the overhead projector lens to be projected onto paper on which the child can color. The children may take turns coloring within the outlined frames. This activity will increase their interest in later coloring at their seats, and they will be more easily motivated to do their best. An opaque projector may be used, but the figures must be placed on a white paper background before they are projected by this projector. The overhead projector may be more easily and effectively used for this activity. It does not require the white paper background (Fig. 37).

Pattern Completion. (a) Children may be directed to draw another shape like the one that is projected onto the "screen." (b) They may draw in parts missing from a projected picture. (c) They may be asked to draw patterns from memory after they were projected.

Capital and lower-case letter introduction of spacing, lines and printing could be supplemented through use with the overhead projector. Construction paper "lines and spaces" may be projected. The children may be helped individually to print letters in their spaces on projected "penmanship paper."

Tracing broken line shapes may be done through the use of construction paper or felt dots used for projection of squares, lines or other simple shapes by the overhead projector. The children may trace their outlined shapes. Left-to-right progression skills can be developed through help for the child individually as he always must begin from the left and trace toward the right as each part of the figure is outlined. For example, if the figure is a square, the child may be instructed to start from the left at the top corner and trace toward the right and down the right side. He may lift his crayon from the paper and come back to the left top, trace down the left side and then trace the bottom from left to right. This help may be given for the purpose of developing skill in eye-hand co-

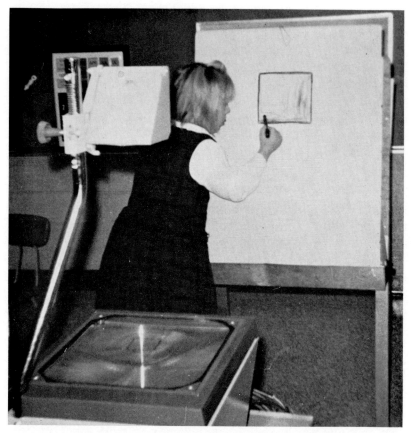

Figure 37. Overhead projector used for coordination skills.

ordination, left-to-right progression and directionality. Activities for tracing figures are contained in pre-reading readiness workbooks. These broken-lined pictures are to be traced by the child as he is given directed help and the needed preparation for the skill of beginning at the left side and moving toward the right, then returning to the designated point before he begins to trace another portion of the outlined picture.

In addition to the suggested preliminary developmental activities in guidebooks for pre-reading programs which involve the use of the chalkboard as an instructional aid, the overhead projector may also be used. This device may be used for introductory activities in which the skill is introduced or to provide supplementary practice and reinforcement exercises. Ample opportunities may be permitted through this media for the children to have mastered the skill before the introduction of their workbook activity.

Auditory Discrimination—The Tape Recorder

A collection of toys that make noise may be used for an activity in which the children are first shown each of the toys and given the opportunity to listen to the noise made by each. A duplicate set of the toys may be placed on a table in front of the children. The teacher may use the other set of toys behind a screen and as each one is caused to make a noise, the children point to the toy on the table that is like the one that made noise. The noises may be recorded on a tape recorder and the children will point to the one on the table that is like the one that made noise as the recorded sounds are heard (Fig. 38).

A tape recorder may be used to record sounds made by animals during a trip to the farm. A culminating activity in the classroom could involve telling what animal made the sound. Familiar sounds heard in the home or at the beach, the train station and others could be recorded and used for other auditory discrimination games.

Sounds of the same type but one loud and one soft may be recorded. As the child listens, he may raise his hand when he hears the loud sound.

Nursery rhymes may be read to the child. As he listens, he may then name the words that rhyme. When the meaning of "words that rhyme" is introduced, those words that rhyme may be emphasized as the teacher says them louder than the rest, such as, "Little Jack *Horner* sat in the *corner*," "Jack and *Jill* went up the *hill*."

Pictures of things that rhyme may be pasted in a row with some that do not rhyme. The child may name those that rhyme. This activity could also be done with the use of the opaque and overhead projectors, flannel board or with three dimensional objects displayed on the Hook N' Loop Board.

Classification—Hook N' Loop or Flannel Boards

Pictures of furniture and other home furnishings for the main

Figure 38. Tape recorder used for auditory discrimination.

rooms in the home are obtainable from catalogs, magazines, or stamp premium catalogs. Inexpensive sets of plastic doll furniture can be purchased at stores. Discussion activities involving ways in which various items of furniture belong in different rooms may be shared by pupils and teacher. The Hook N' Loop Board may be divided into sections and labels such as "kitchen," "dining room," or "bedroom" may be prepared and placed at the top of each section. The children will then place the pictures or three dimensional furniture in the room section where it is most likely to belong. They may discuss how some kinds of furniture such as chairs, lamps, and others are used in various rooms.

Association and Relationship—Projectors

Pictures of objects or three dimensional objects may be matched with those with which they should be used.

A page of pictures could be prepared for use with the opaque or overhead projectors (on transparencies for overhead). Real items that are used with the pictured ones may be held up one by one for pupil observation and the question asked, "What is this used with?" (a light bulb). The children will find the pictured lamp and tell how they are used together.

Pages with "key" pictures at the top and others at the bottom could be prepared so that the children may point to the picture at the bottom or tell how it is used with the top one. (Example: A pillow may be the key picture at the top. The child will find, among other pictures, one of a blanket at the bottom and indicate it and tell about its association with blanket.)

Picture Meanings—Opaque Projector

Pictures that suggest a story that can be told by the children may be cut from magazines and other sources. They may be mounted on a construction paper background to be projected. The children may tell stories or answer questions about them. Simple pictures that require the answer to a very easy question would be used with the slower learners. This activity is very helpful to them in gaining the ability to use language to describe or tell something as well as learning to use complete sentences, observe details and grasp pictured meanings.

Vocabulary and the use of verbal skills seems to be an area in which there is a great lack of facility shown by some first graders in the pre-reading stage.

Picture Recognition—Hand-made Tachistoscopic Device

Tachistoscopic devices are recommended by Doctor Kathleen Hester for word drills. She described how these devices may be made from favorite pictures chosen by the children cut out and mounted on tagboard or cardboard.[60]

---

[60]Kathleen B. Hester: *Teaching Every Child To Read.* © 1948, 1955, p. 164. Courtesy of Harper & Row, Publishers, New York.

Tachistoscopic devices may also be used in reading readiness for providing the child with the opportunity to quickly name pictures as they come through the view opening of the hand-made tachistoscopic device. Such instructional aids may be made from two pieces of tagboard. A view opening could be cut in the front piece of the tagboard and covered with cellophane or plastic. The sides are fastened with staples or masking tape. The ends are left open for the strip of pictures to be pulled through for viewing. Another tachistoscopic device prepared from a carton has been described (Fig. 39).

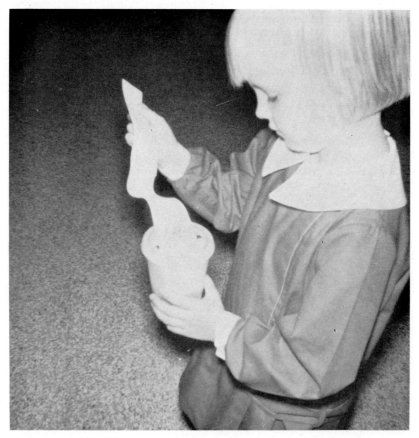

Figure 39. Handmade tachistoscopic device for picture recognition.

This device could also be used with "reels" to contain items for the child to indicate likenesses and differences.

Comparison of Shape and Serial Order

Children must be able to match groupings according to serial order if they are to be ready for the complex skill of remembering words that are similar at the beginning, in the middle or at the end. This matching ability must first be acquired concerning pictures during the readiness period before the child is confronted with the additional task of remembering words and their likenesses and differences at various portions, such as *end* and *middle*. During a summer school remedial reading period, a record was kept of some words which were confusing to the children. Each word seemed to have a "mate" that was similar and the two were confusing to the children because of their similarity. The list of confusing word mates include the following:

last and *lost*	*back* and *black*	*ran* and *run*
first and *fast*	*was* and *saw*	*walk* and *walked*
then and *them*	*paint* and *painted*	*let* and *lot*
us and *as*	*made* and *make*	*his* and *has*
ate and *eat*	*give* and *gave*	*read* and *reading*
wish and *which*	*but* and *put*	*of* and *for*
every and *very*	*how* and *now*	*think* and *thank*
fell and *fall*	*fine* and *fire*	*out* and *cut*
home and *house*	*horse* and *house*	*store* and *story*
at and *ate*	*went* and *want*	*on* and *no*
read and *road*	*begin* and *began*	*wish* and *wash*
form and *from*	*party* and *pretty*	*snow* and *show*

There were other troublesome and confusing words, but this list represents many that were most often confused by the children who needed remedial help. It seems that a more prolonged and reinforced experience background in the skill of comparing and noting likenesses and differences in serial order during the reading readiness period would better prepare the children to cope with these problem words in their reading. Other reading skills, such as the use of initial and final consonant sounds and other word-attack skills are also needed. Reading is so complex that a variety of skills are being used simultaneously whether or not the reader is aware of this. This causes the necessity for the instructor to prepare the child through provision for mastery of as many skills possible in the readiness stage to help smooth out the reading path. The faster learners master these skills quickly and seem to take to reading "as a duck takes to water," but the remedial reading classes are filled with those pupils who must plod laboriously uphill and need help every step of the way.

There are activity pages in various readiness workbooks that involve matching pictures according to shape and order in groupings. Three picture groupings on the left side of the page include three kinds of picture series that are alternately placed in a different position in each grouping. A certain pictured object may be first in one group and last in another. These picture rows may be as follows:

Row one: tree, house, boat
Row two: house, tree, boat
Row Three: boat, tree, house

The same order is followed concerning the groupings on the right, but their row positions are changed so that the child must match each grouping on the left with one that is exactly the same on the right. This requires mature ability to scrutinize, remember and match. The pictures in rows on the left to be matched with their corresponding ones on the right may appear as follows:

tree, house, boat	house, tree, boat
house, tree, boat	boat, tree, house
boat, tree, house	tree, house, boat

Visual equipment to be used as supplementary activities to prepare the children for these skills are listed.

1. *Flannel Board*. Felt shapes or picture arrangements may be matched according to serial order.

2. *Pegboard*. Peg arrangements varied in color may be matched in serial order according to color or position.

3. *Sponge Shapes*. May be arranged in serial order positions on the magnetic board or flannel board. Small magnets may be placed in the center of sponge shapes through carefully cut openings, and they will adhere to the magnetic board "magically," according to the children.

4. *Thin foam rubber* may be used for preparing shapes that will adhere to the flannel board.

5. *Overhead Projector*. Felt figures may be used. They will project as an opaque dark shape, but can be used according to shape, not color. Special transparencies may be prepared.

6. *Arrangements* of blocks, plastic spoons, small toys, or other three-dimensional objects may be prepared in rows on a table or desk so that groupings on the left may be matched with those on the right. Children may be encouraged to bring in their prizes from "Cracker jacks" for use with this activity.

Each piece of audiovisual equipment has a valuable contribution to make to teaching whether it be instrumental in introducing an entirely new media of instruction or is built upon the principle involved in some other device but offers a means through which a new technique is possible. Many of the seemingly new ideas and possible approaches through instructional materials are the descendants of some device or technique that has been used by teachers in the past who have been continually striving to develop every possible means to meet a pupil need. Many other new materials are available through the efforts of the Federal Government, and are more readily possible now through the advancement in the industrial research which provides more inexpensive materials for their manufacture.

Teachers today have available more instructional materials for use in their classrooms than they have ever had before, but the need is greater for creative teaching, wise choice of instructional media, and the devising of means through which all of these aids can be made available for pupil learning. More realization of pupil needs necessitates teacher preparation of instructional aids planned for that unique need. There may be a danger of permitting the instructional materials to be applied too generally since there are so many available. The need exists for purposeful utilization of instructional materials and direct application of audivisual aids to the achievement of learning aims and instructional purposes.

Every instructional aid offers advantages and important contributions, but it also requires teacher evaluation and application to pupil needs as well as preliminary preparation of instructional materials if others are needed to supplement it. There must also be teacher planning of techniques and experimentation with a variety of media. Continued evaluation of instructional media and techniques can be helpful to individual teachers as well as provide valuable findings and observations to be shared with others.

Every audiovisual aid, no matter how versatile or complex, must be applied to the instructional purpose as realized by the teacher and needed by the learner. Needed provision for the aid to be supplemented with the use of others or used again in a variety of ways to provide repetition and review must be considered when this is necessary.

Audiovisual aids do not necessarily promise easier methods of instruction, but they offer more channels and greatly effective means through which pupil success, motivation and inspiration can be achieved.*

---

*The felt board drills for "Ability to See Differences" are from "Language Development for the Trainable" by Mary Lou Durbin, *The Pointer for Special Class Teachers and Parents of the Handicapped* (Vol. II, No. 2, 1966, p. 47. The Association for Special Class Teachers and Parents of the Handicapped, Inc.).

Chapter XIII

RESEARCH IMPLICATIONS FOR THE
TRAINABLE CHILD*

T HERE EXISTS the need for educators to be continually aware of new research findings and their implications for curriculum planning to meet the needs of the trainable mentally handicapped children in special classes.

Curriculum planning must include effort to meet their present immediate needs and also provide for their future, yet serve as a tool for educators to use in realizing and keeping abreast of new findings significant to student learning possibilities.

Williams emphasizes the need for more knowledge concerning trainable children, how they learn, and the best ways of teaching them.[61] They have all of the needs of childhood plus many fears that other children do not have to contend with. Effort is needed to find better ways to communicate with trainable children, learn how they feel about themselves, and to counsel them.

Some research studies reported in the educational journals reflect the growing realization of the need to provide for their individual differences, limited though their potential may be.

> Slowly we are recognizing the distinctive features of our children and appreciating the diversity within the group. Instead of viewing them as the "below fifty group" or as the "trainable" or as the "severely retarded," we have begun to see children— children with serious problems arising from a variety of causes yielding to a variety of approaches. We are addressing ourselves to the uniqueness of each child. We are asking ourselves not

---

*Part of a review of research presented by the author at the Conference for Personnel in Programs for the Trainable Mentally Handicapped sponsored by the Michigan Department of Public Instruction at Walden Woods Camp, Hartland, Michigan May 7-8, 1965.

[61]From Harold M. Williams, *loc. cit.*

what is his IQ, but in what way Johnny or Mary or Peter is attempting with his limited resources to meet the challenge of his everyday living and how we can help Johnny or Mary or Peter meet them more appropriately and more effectively.[62]

The Training School Bulletin (1958) stressed the need for initiative, ingenuity and imagination in the teacher's approach to make the most of each child's abilities. These "3 I's" are needed if the key to help each child is to be found by the teacher.[63]

Classroom Research

Classroom action research and experimentation with methods and materials are valuable means whereby the special education teacher may become more aware of the use of these devices and techniques to find solutions to curriculum problems.

The teacher of trainable children is confronted with the need to understand and endeavor to help the children who constitute a garden variety of clinical types of mental retardation. Included in the class group may be brain-injured and other severely retarded children such as those afflicted with mongolism, microcephaly, and cretinism. Many are hindered by emotional distrurbances and communicative difficulties. Their physical disabilities may include severe cardiac conditions, and auditory, visual and speech handicaps. Some of the children may be extremely hyperactive and restless while others may require special motivation and stimulation.

It is difficult to provide any one environment to meet each peculiar need of all clinical types. However, we are challenged to provide for individual differences in every possible way. The teacher must evaluate and utilize research that has been done and consider the findings and their implications. The teacher also must do further research in education to provide instructional aids for children with limitations.

---

[62]From Louis Rosenzweig: How far have we come? *American Journal of Mental Deficiency,* July, 1959, Vol. 64, No. 1, p. 13.

[63]From Harold Delp, Ph.D.: The 3 I's, not the 3 R's; teachers of mentally retarded. *The Training School Bulletin,* May, 1958, Vol. 55, No. 1 pp. 11-14. Courtesy of the Training School Unit of the American Institute for Mental Studies Vineland, New Jersey.

Action research using a variety of instructional materials will aid the teacher in devising teaching aids which will accomplish the instructional aim and provide for the handicap and the learning difficulty of the learner.[64]

Extensive research projects involving many children in different programs and observed responses of students to various techniques, teacher personalities and the many other factors in learning are very necessary, but the need for the classroom teacher to attempt to systematically solve problems as they are realized must not be ignored. Researchers may realize the general needs of trainable children, but the classroom teacher is the one who may be most aware of the individual differences and personal needs of the students as they are found in particular classroom situations.

The need to help the trainable retarded has always existed whether it was realized or not, but today many teachers have more opportunities and instructional materials as well as resource people to help in the realization of the aim—the very necessary aim to develop the abilities of each child to the extent of his potential and to help him to more profitably work and play with others. Classroom research can be an outstanding aspect of curriculum planning in this vast, exciting field of educational endeavor.

Instructional aims have become more apparent and goals have needed to become identified and defined since the acceptance of the responsibilities that accompany the planning of programs and classroom procedures for the trainable child. There exists a greater need than merely training the child to adjust to one life routine. Living, even in a closely supervised and structured environment, permits emergencies to arise with their needs for new adjustments that present challenges and opportunities for growth, also. Ways may be sought through research to educate the children to meet changes or to make necessary adjustments, be adequate in emergencies and assume responsibilities for themselves and each other whenever possible.

Trainable retarded children, as do all members of a classroom group, display a range of individual interests, differences and

---

[64]From Mary Lou Durbin and Clement L. Kaye: Materials and the severely retarded. *Michigan Education Journal,* March 1, 1963, Volume XL, Number 14, p. 501. Courtesy of The Michigan Education Association.

abilities. They differ in what they can learn, and length of time required for learning as well as in their responses to instructional techniques and materials. Some children have other needs due to their possible additional physical handicaps, such as cardiac weaknesses. These problems affect their attendance in school, especially during the winter months, and create the need for the school program to be adjusted accordingly.

The variety of clinical types represented in the trainable class creates the need for instruction and materials to be evaluated and applied in accordance with the child needs.

Research may enable educators to continually evaluate pupil needs and keep goals high as well as realistic in possibility of accomplishment. Although much insight has been gained concerning the retarded children, too little is still realized in regard to the learning abilities and unique needs of the severely handicapped children in the trainable classification. Awareness of their limitations is necessary, but through research, another kind of danger can be alleviated: The danger of not challenging the learner sufficiently and keeping expectations high enough to require his best effort.

A paper representing a review of experimental studies of learning in mentally deficient persons stated the following in the summary.

> Some papers highlight a slow, arduous learning process among mental defectives whereas others point to more skill in acquisition than is ordinarily assumed. There is evidence that intellectual level is not an adequate predictor of the learning of mental defectives and their learning *per se* is variable.[65]

Another supporting source also seems to suggest the need for continued research with the following:

> Many studies have reported low or zero correlations between intelligence test scores and learning task performance.[66]

---

[65]From Marion White McPherson: Learning and mental deficiency. *The American Journal of Mental Deficiency*, March, 1958, Vol. 62, No. 5, p. 877. Courtesy of The American Association on Mental Deficiency.

[66]From Betty L. House and David Zeaman: Visual discrimination learning and intelligence in defectives of low mental age. *The American Journal of Mental Deficiency*, July, 1960, Vol. 65, p. 51.

The Curriculum Research Committee of the Michigan Curriculum Program sponsored by the Michigan Department of Public Instruction stresses the solving of classroom problems through classroom action research carried out by the teacher. The Committee's guidebook, *Solving Classroom Problems Through Systematic Study,* presents basic principles for classroom action research and the evaluation of findings and their implications. The following suggested steps in action research are provided by the Committee:

Questions To Help You Solve Your Classroom Problems

You have many instructional problems you'd like to solve. This is where research starts—with a feeling of dissatisfaction. Perhaps you have some hunches you'd like to test. How can you do it? A good way to start is by asking yourself some questions.

1. *What is the most important problem I need to solve?*
   Why do I feel I need to solve this problem?
   (a.) How is it important to me?
   (b.) How will its solution affect the improvement of educational experiences for children in my classroom?

2. *Can I state this problem more specifically?*
   (a.) Is this problem made up of several smaller problems? If so, I feel the most important subproblem is, State it specifically and keep it simple.
   (b.) Am I certain that I know what the terms I use mean? (Write your definition of the terms.)
   (c.) Am I certain that my objectives for the program are clear? State them briefly. (Do I hope these youngsters will gain added knowledge? Master certain skills? Develop new attitudes? Which ones specifically?)

3. *What are some hunches (hypotheses) I have about how to solve the problem?*
   ("I'll bet if I—then so and so would happen.")
   a. Choose the hypothesis you feel promises to have the greatest impact on improving learning for your children.

4. *How and from whom can I get the information I need to test my hypothesis?*
   a. What do I already know about the specific problem and its solution?

    b. What have others found out about the problem?
    c. From whom should the information come? When do I gather this information? How can I get the information I need? By observation? (If so, state behavior expected.) By questionnaire or other instrument? (Homemade or commercial?)

Once you have gone this far you have your study designed. You know what your problem is, you've designed it specifically, you have a hunch to test, and you know how you will get the information you need to test your hunch. Only three steps remain, and they are important steps.

5. You will next *gather the information* you have decided is necessary and record it carefully.

6. It will then be necessary to *analyze the information* you have collected. You will probably organize the results in a manner which will make for ease of handling and analysis; then you will determine what the facts are from the data you've gathered.

7. Lastly you will *draw conclusions from the results* of your study and, if you feel it necessary, *state now hunches or hypotheses* which need to be tested.

That's the action research process. Any problem, simple or complex, can be studied using the steps just stated.

Steps in the Action Research Process

1. Select your problem.
2. Define the problem specifically.
3. State the hunches (hypothoses) you wish to test.
4. Develop methods for testing your hunches.
5. Gather the facts.
6. Organize and analyze the facts.
7. Draw conclusions and propose new hypotheses if necessary.

Remember the hunches you tested are those important to you and the results will be primarily for your use. Nevertheless, you will find it necessary to keep a written record of your statement of the problem and the data you collected for your own use, perhaps, to share with your fellow workers.[67]

---

[67]*Solving Classroom Problems Through Systematic Study.* Curriculum Research Committee of the Michigan Curriculum Program Bulletin, No. 433, pp. 2-3. The Department of Public Instruction Lansing, Michigan. Courtesy of The Michigan Department of Education.

Chapter XIV

RECOMMENDATIONS FOR READINESS

R ESEARCH STUDIES and critical evaluation of children's reading problems are supportive of the need for a more thorough and prolonged readiness program to help those who are not ready to read at the time of first grade entrance.

> Hoggard warns, "One of the chief causes of reading failure is rushing children in the initial reading program before they are ready."[68]

This writer's recommendations for early involvement of parents at the child's preschool and first grade level were presented. The need was emphasized for the school to lead the way in communication of curriculum goals to parents through conferences and a special handbook to be prepared by the school personnel for the parents. This handbook may contain recommendations and suggestions concerning parent sponsored home readiness preparation.

Effort to prevent failures in reading through adequate diagnosis of pupil needs during the readiness period and the provision of sufficient time and instruction for this remediation should be proportionate to the provision for later remedial measures which are usually applied in cases of reading difficulties. All school reading programs should include emphasis upon prevention of reading difficulties through sufficient readiness as well as diagnosis and remediation of existing reading difficulties.

Bond and Tinker present a warning concerning the price paid by pupil failures in reading if adequate provisions are not made for needed success in the readiness areas.

---

[68]Kendall J. Hoggard: Readiness is the best prevention. *Readings on Reading Instruction,* Edited by Albert J. Harris. David McKay Company, Inc., New York, © 1963, p. 69. Originally printed in *Education,* LXXVII (May, 1957), pp. 523-27. Reprinted by courtesy of the author and the Bobbs-Merrill Co., Indianapolis, Indiana.

Reading disability is frequently caused by starting a child in a standard reading program before he has acquired the readiness which will assure success in classroom reading activities. Due to his lack of experience, verbal facility, intellectual or emotional maturity, or a combination of these, he is unable to achieve enough of the learnings day by day to handle satisfactorily what is coming next. Inability to cope with the assignments produces frustration which leads to feelings of inadequacy, inferiority, insecurity, and perhaps even rebellion.

The large incidence of failures in reading during the primary grades is due in part to lack of reading readiness. Any educational program or administrative policy which provides the same formal reading instruction for all pupils at the beginning of grade one can only lead to disaster for many pupils.[69]

Teachers of first graders find these most common pupil problems at the beginning of the first grade school year:

1. Lack of ability to concentrate purposefully.
2. Inability to follow specific oral directions. This is often especially so if the directions contain any length or if they involve more than one direction. A teacher who told her pupils, "Put away your workbooks and crayons first, and then you may wait at the door to go out and play", reported that ten or twelve children who apparently heard only the last part of the direction immediately lined up at the door, leaving their things on their desks. This indicated the need for instructive help in learning to listen and follow directions.
3. Few independent work skills. Many children, even when they are given a choice of activity, cannot plan purposefully or complete self-directed tasks.
4. Lack of skills in handling tools, scissors, pencils, etc.
5. Lack of conceptual vocabulary caused by an insufficient experiential background.
6. Inability to classify, make generalizations, or verbally tell why things belong together or may not belong to a group. This is found especially so if the likenesses or differences are more ab-

[69]Guy L. Bond and Miles A. Tinker, *loc. cit.,* p. 115.

stract, involve no specific "right" or "wrong" answers, but may be dependent upon how they may be considered according to how the child can utilize his experiential background to interpret and explain his conclusions.

7. Extremely short spans of interest and attention.

8. Lack of student self-confidence in their ability to follow directions or complete tasks without seeking almost continual approval or directions from the teacher.

9. Poor motor and eye-hand coordination skills.

10. Lack of perceptual development.

Systematic effort in accordance with teacher awareness of growth in the sequential steps can help to reveal and identify many skills in which individual students may be more successful and those in which they lack competency. After using the readiness materials described in the earlier chapter, the teacher of the kindergarten class remarked, "One fact that this activity project has revealed to me is that the slower learners can do better in many skills than I had thought they could, and their weak areas have been identified." Apparently the self-confidence gained by the children, their interest in the variety of devices and activities, and the short easy tasks involved were factors that influenced their performance.

Diagnosis of pupil performance according to skill areas may be helpful in making recommendations to the child's next teacher. Broad generalizations, such as, "He is immature," or "She is not adjusting," cannot provide the constructive aid that the new teacher needs in diagnosing the pupil's needs and planning for their fulfillment. More help may be offered by listing in detail some individual skill achievement and the child's weak areas. The readiness and pre-reading program can be one of pupil need appraisal, and recommendations for helping the child to get off to the best possible start in reading. Diagnostic procedures by the kindergarten teacher in the latter part of the year will offer assistance also in determining the skills and other learning areas in which the student may need additional time, repetition and change of skill introduction and reinforcement, as well as measures to provide the needed experiential and informational background for concept-building. Definite suggested areas in which the child lacks skill and the kindergarten teacher's recommendations will be invaluable during the child's preparation for reading in the first grade.

Standardized readiness tests are usually administered at the end of the kindergarten year or more often after the students have entered first grade subsequent to a few weeks of reading readiness instruction. Purposes for administering such tests are usually to determine the student's readiness status and for use in determining what additional help is needed. Some tests, such as the Ginn Pre-reading Tests, also offer suggested remedial procedures for the teacher to use with students who lack certain readiness competencies.

Perhaps testing may also be helpful if used with the instructional aspect of the readiness program through the media of teacher devised informal readiness tests to determine extent of pupil achievement involving specific skills and concepts. Teacher devised readiness tests may provide guidelines for the teacher's use in diagnosing and understanding pupil difficulties in readiness skill areas. Just as testing is one helpful tool used in determining other learning needs in reading, it may also have a contribution to be made to the prevention of reading difficulties through its application during the readiness stage.

Apparently if more diagnostic and remedial measures were carried out during the readiness period and more time were permitted for needed individual help, much pupil exposure to reading failures may be avoided. Johnson stresses the need for readiness and the importance of time being taken for its development as he writes:

> Readiness is an extreremly important phase of instruction in the development of any skill or concept. Time spent preparing children for instruction will be more than repaid in the rapidity with which the learning will be acquired. Healthy attitudes will also be developed toward learning and socially more acceptable overt behavior will result. The children are having success. There is no necessity for the development of socially unacceptable, compensatory behavior.[70]

A teacher-prepared readiness test may consist of individual

---

[70]Orville G. Johnson: *Education for the Slow Learners.* © 1963, p. 310. Reprinted by permission of Prentice-Hall, Inc., Englewood Cliffs, New Jersey.

items concerning the skill areas. The testing devices may include a variety of materials. The techniques may involve verbal responses, manipulative activities, projective types of answers that concern the child's individual background of experiences and activities that challenge pupil creativity. Some written skills may be included, such as marking items with a pencil or crayon, but there may also be provision for individual oral responses. Some of the testing activities may also be done with small groups of children, and others may include individual tasks to be done at the child's seat independently.

Too often, a short attention or interest span may hinder a child from really doing his best on a standardized test. There is often too much repetition of response types and the techniques involved. The testing situation becomes wearisome to some children, and the desire to get it over with becomes the chief goal. A readiness test should contain motivating and interesting items that will sustain pupil interest to the extent that he will want to do his best throughout the procedure. The teacher's observations during the testing period and the comments of the children may also be very pertinent and worthy of consideration.

Informal teacher testing may also provide opportunities for children to comment, ask questions and express their thoughts and impressions. Testing that is done infrequently and during which the otherwise very helpful teacher who is willing to answer questions must not now make any comments, but merely directs the child to work independently may create a tense atmosphere that prohibits the most confident or competent work of some anxious children. The insecure children need many varied and interesting opportunities to work by themselves and learn to respond to testing confidently. This cannot be done if so much emphasis is placed upon pupil performance during one or two testing experiences during the year and the child either feels pressure and stress or gives up without really trying.

Materials for test-item preparation may be obtained from many sources, including certain pages from readiness workbooks which involve certain skills, pictures from magazines, catalogs, inexpensive picture books, teacher prepared items to be used with the audiovisual equipment, and other sources. Merely flat media should not be used, but there should be three dimensional objects included for use. Small blocks and miniature toys may be used for counting, matching activities, comparing, and others. This creates additional opportunities for the testing of pupils' manipulative ability and coordination skills in a variety of settings.

Testing should reveal what the child has experienced and how well he can express what he has gained from these experiences. This revelation can be accomplished more fully if there is provision to permit expression of the individual's perception as determined by his experiences and their influence. This may be considered in the evaluation of informal test results. A child who was responding to a standardized test was directed to "mark the spool of thread." Since this was an individual test situation, more freedom was permitted for the student to talk the teacher. He remarked that he would ". . . not mark anything because there wasn't any thread there." The teacher, attempting to understand the thinking that had influenced his conclusion, asked him to name the pictured objects in the row. The child did so, describing the spool of thread as "wire like I used to fix my bike." The large pictured spool did resemble one of wire more than thread. What is revealed concerning the child's experiences and how he applies them can be very significant in readiness instruction.

Informal testing for skill mastery can be especially helpful if the items are presented through more than one media and in various settings. Audiovsiual aids, such as filmstrips, those items viewed through the media of the opaque and overhead projectors, charts, flat pictures, three-dimensional objects, and other real objects cause the retesting of the same items to be a possible new and exciting challenge presented in a variety of interesting situations. Something new may be revealed relating to the child's learning needs each time the items are used, or the teacher may make different or more pertinent observations through a broader understanding of the child's readiness needs.

Purposeful planning, changing or revising instructional aids and techniques, are more readily possible through teacher prepared informal testing. Such continuous creative devising, preparing, and changing of instructional aids are necessary to *help this child to learn this skill in this way* because *this help seems best for the individual.*

Informal testing can not in any way replace the need for standardized testing or detract at all from its value. The standardized tests that have been proven both valid and reliable through their continued effective use with many representative students are very necessary and serve both diagnostic and remedial purposes. The suggestion contained herein for additional informal testing is given merely as another possible medium by which preventive and remedial readiness may be accomplished. The value of such teacher effort to seek better ways to meet even one learning need of one pupil cannot be overemphasized.

I. Questions Relating to How Well the Child Can Express a Broad Knowledge of Personal Background Information:
    A. His full name, address and phone number.
    B. The names of the members of his family.
    C. His knowledge of the names of the general areas of the body and facial features including such more detailed names as shin, elbow, forearm, etc.
    D. Ability to name articles of clothing.
    E. Ability to name toys, things for work, furniture, dishes, items of silverware, things that belong in the kitchen, etc.
    F. Ability to name objects in relation to more general or abstract classifications, such as:
        1. Names three things that are always found outdoors.
        2. Name five toys that boys like, etc.
    G. Naming pets, farm and zoo animals and being able to classify them.
    H. Naming fruits and vegetables, indicating them by pointing to those named by the teacher, and being able to classify them as directed.
    I. Giving the names of machinery (construction, farm, etc.)
    J. Naming vehicles for transportation.
    K. Color recognition.
    L. Recognition of general pictured items or miniature objects, etc.

M. Telling how pictured objects may be used.

II. Personal or Self-care Skills:

A. Ability to manage one's own coat, snowsuit, boots, etc.

B. Ability to tie own shoes.

C. Care of shoes.

D. Ability to keep one's own room neat, put toys away, make bed, etc.

E. Ability to put things away in a cupboard or rows of shelves and to have understanding of the concepts of *top, middle* and *bottom* shelves.

F. Ability to brush one's own teeth, wash hands and face, dress self, use a handkerchief and other personal skills.

III. Verbal Skills:

A. Ability to express one's statements clearly and distinctly.

B. Ability to express thoughts or ideas in complete sentences.

C. Ability to ask questions that are related to a subject and to answer questions appropriately.

D. Ability to describe action, feelings and experiences shown in simple pictures.

E. Ability to retell a sequence of pictured events or those involved in a simple story that the child has heard.

F. Can answer questions relating to action sequences, such as, "Where did Jack look first before he finally found Spotty in the barn?"

G. Can give reasons or draw conclusions from one's own observations of pictures or actions in story pictures or film-strip illustrations.

IV. Questions Relating to the Child's Understanding of His Own Environment:

A. Ability to recognize or name things in his environment that have been experienced or otherwise exposed to by the child.

B. Ability to share experiences, tell about them or include them in dramatized demonstrations.

C. Enjoyment of or understanding of simple songs and poetry.

D. Realization of humorous or sad events, actions, etc. as depicted by pictures or stories.

E. Ability to understand and relate order of pictured story sequences.

V. Questions Relating to Knowledge of Safety Skills, Social Skills, Meeting Emergencies and Health Habits:

A. Knowledge of what to do or whom to ask for help in case of being lost.

B. Telling what should be done in case of described emergency situations, such as fire or sickness.

C. How to cross a street safely.

D. How to dress carefully for outdoor play in winter.

E. What to remember when going swimming.

VI. Coordination Skills:

A. Physical coordination activities involving gross motor and large muscle skills.

    1. Walking on patterns.

    2. Bouncing a ball on patterns.

    3. Bouncing a ball continuously, throwing, catching, etc.

    4. Running and skipping.

    5. Playing with a ball to knock down tenpins, playing ring toss in a variety of games.

B. Finer muscular skill activities.

    1. Coloring, tracing, and use of scissors.

    2. Pasting and completing manipulative seatwork tasks.

C. Perceptual skills.

    1. Completing simple matching puzzles in a variety of settings.

    2. Completing pegboard designs.

    3. Reproducing a figure or shape, pattern completion and drawing in missing parts.

    4. Ability to visualize parts missing from pictures.

VII. Ability To Distinguish and Determine Conceptual Meanings:

A. Meanings of big and little, up and down, here and there, first and last, tall and short, over and under, middle, top and bottom, and large and small, etc.

B. Ability to interpret conceptual meanings and describe them in appropriate vocabulary.

VIII. Ability To See Relationships:
A. Associating two or three pictures from a series and telling why they are related.
B. Choosing which picture may belong in a series.
C. Describing more general associations of pictures, such as three people who may be community helpers as shown in the pictured grouping.

IX. Classification:
A. Classifying fruits and vegetables, zoo and farm animals, things for work and play, etc.
B. Classification of things according to use, size, action, etc.

X. Conceptual Vocabulary:
A. Indicating the picture that illustrates the given verbal description.
B. Recognition of named objects in a picture series.
C. Recognition of pictures or objects according to their described use, such as, "Find the thing that we live in" or "Find what we can ride in," etc.

XI. Auditory Discrimination:
A. Ability to recognize sounds made by toys, animals, familiar musical or rhythm instruments, etc.
B. Counting sounds heard, such as listening and counting how many times a ball is bounced even though it is concealed from view.
C. Ability to indicate rhyming words as nursery rhymes or songs are heard.
D. Indication of rhyming pictures in a series.

XII. Listening Skills:
A. Ability to purposefully listen as directed.
1. Listening for words that describe actions or noises.
2. Listening and playing a musical instrument at the designated time.
3. Listening for refrains or repeated words in songs or poems.

B. Listening and performing when two directions are given in a sentence, such as, "Put the red book away, then open the door."

C. Listening for and following directions that have a time interval between each, such as "Put the reading books in the cupboard then get the chairs ready for a filmstrip story."

D. Remembering directions after a period of time, such as, "Let the filmstrip projector get cool while we are using the puzzles. Put the lid back on later."

XIII. Associating Comprehensive Word Meanings with Their Pictures:

A. Indicating the proper picture from a series in response to one descriptive word, such as: Indicating a banana in response to the word "fruit."

B. Associating sentence meanings: "Find the thing that tells time."

XIV. Discrimination of Differences:

A. Gross and finer visual discrimination.

B. Sensory differences, such as, "Which one is sweet?" in a row of pictures.

C. Differences in meanings: "What is for work?" in a row of pictures.

    1. What goes up high?

    2. What is found on the ground?

    3. Who grows tall?

    4. Which is short? Long?

D. Letter differences.

    1. Capitals and lower-case.

    2. Differences in words.

E. Opposites in meaning.

XV. Indicating Likenesses:

A. Pictures.

B. Shapes.

C. Capital and lower-case letters.

E. Color words.

XVI. Recognition of Association:
   A. Pictured object presentations, such as:
      1. A fork and its association with a dish in a pictured series.
      2. A hat and its association with another article of clothing in the series.
   B. Ability to describe or explain these associations.

XVII. Left-to-right Progression Skill:
   A. Ability to "read" a row of pictures with the return sweep needed in left-to-right progression.
   B. Ability to follow "rows" or not lose one's place in the pictured rows.
   C. Remembering to begin at left each time.

XVIII. Discrimination of Serial Order:
   A. Ability to match rows containing two or three pictures or shapes on the left side with their corresponding rows on the right.
   B. Ability to match these in a variety of settings such as pegboard rows, flannel board drills, etc.
   C. Ability to complete seatwork activities involving drawing lines or pasting according to serial order.

XIX. Independent Work Skills:
   A. Ability to stay with a task and anticipate its completion.
   B. Ability to work with small groups of other children.
   C. Ability to work independently.
   D. Ability to make purposeful use of spare or free time.

These general guidelines have been offered for suggested use by the teacher in preparing informal readiness tests as aids in evaluating the pre-reader's readiness status. They cover some of the broader skill areas, and may be applied in accordance with pupil needs and the curriculum goals considered by the teacher. They may also be helpful when used in testing for the purpose of continuous development of instructional materials designed for changing learner needs or as growth and development become apparent in different skill areas.

There exists a wide range of differences in philosophy concerning the areas to be emphasized in the kindergarten programs. Some educators stress the social and emotional goals and provision for them in kindergarten and oppose formal reading readiness at that instructional level. Many of these activities, however, such as creative play, socialization experiences, finger-painting, use of clay and many others that are utilized in kindergarten classes are also activities to promote aspects of reading readiness.

There are, however, the subskills that must be provided for in getting the child ready for readiness. The purpose here has been to offer possible helpful suggestions for providing the needed background that may prepare the child for success in readiness skills.

The faster learner has acquired this preparatory background so smoothly that the growth is often not visible, but its evidence exists in the child's success and self-confidence. This child who is ready and eager to read at the beginning of first grade or possibly even in kindergarten, can easily sail through the basic readers and enjoy supplementary books at the end of the year and eagerly visit the library. The needs of the children who are delayed in these necessary skills cannot be fulfilled by rigid adherence to grade levels, imposition of formal reading instruction, lack of needed time to achieve at each skill level and insufficient repetition of readiness skill and concept building activities.

Some authorities suggest the services of the junior or pre-first-grade room for children who seem to need a continued readiness program at the end of kindergarten. Others recommend the junior primary classes in which much individual help may also be given according to pupil growth and needs. The Head Start programs which sponsor preschool readiness experiences for the disadvantaged children are designed to prevent much of the reading retardation resulting from lack of language growth, very little conceptual development and undeveloped cognitive thinking skill.

A possible flexible plan which seems adaptable by most school systems for meeting the needs of the child found delayed in the readiness skills is the provision of readiness teachers who may work with the groups of children in the different buildings within the school system. This is similar in plan of instruction to the remedial reading program which provides for the correction of reading handicaps, but this plan offers possible prevention of difficulties.

The children who may be referred for this teacher's services may be screened after the kindergarten teacher's observations are considered as well as when the results of reading readiness testing are available. The readiness teacher would work with small groups of children during the latter part of the kindergarten and throughout the first grade years, and may also provide supplementary materials and suggested techniques for classroom instruction in consultation with the child's regular teacher. Perhaps this type of preventive procedure may make a contribution to the success of the child who is delayed in the readiness skills.

Experiences which the child has lacked may be provided also through this type of service. Bus trips involving several groups of children from different buildings may be arranged through the classroom teacher's observations as well as those of the readiness teacher's realization of pupil needs. Funds should be made available for this type of service to the small but significant group of children who are found in many first grade classrooms.

APPENDIX

INSTRUCTIONAL MATERIAL AND SOURCES

THESE RECOMMENDED materials for use in pre-reading instruction are grouped according to the type of media which they represent. Some special recommendations for application of the instructional materials to the learning needs are included.

Instructional Books for Teacher Use

1. Ellis, Mary Jackson: *Kindergarten Rhymes* with flannel cutouts. Book and cutouts, available from F.A. Owen Publishing Co.

2. Ellis, Mary J.: *Manipulative Language Arts.* For all grades. This includes specific suggestions for nonreading activities at the lower grade level, guidance in development in relation to reading readiness, concept enrichment, language activities, visual games, sequential thinking, motor activities, audio and speech, left to right, and work habits. Each book $1.95. Available from Teachers Publishing Corporation Darien, Connecticut (06820).

3. Long, Paul E.: *Teaching With the Flannel Board.* Price $1.50. Available from Instructo Products Co. 1635 North 55th St., Philadelphia 31, Pennsylvania.

4. Scott, Louis Binder, and Thompson, J.J.: *Rhymes for Fingers and Flannelboards* (c. 1960). $4.48. Available from Webster Division McGraw-Hill Book Co., 1154 Reco Avenue, St. Louis, Missouri (63126).

5. Scott, Louis Binder: *Stories That Stick on the Flannelboard.* The Instructor Handbook Series. F.A. Owen Publishing Co., Dansville, New York (c. 1959).

6. Scott, Louis Binder, and Thompson, J.J.: *Talking Time.* For speech and listening in the primary grades. $3.76. Available from the same source as Number Four.

Audiovisual Materials

Flannel or Felt Board Instructional Aids

Available from Instructo Products Co., 1635 North 55th St., Philadelphia 31, Pennsylvania.

1. *The Farm*, No. 87. Cutouts of farm buildings, machinery and people.
2. *Farm Animals*, No. 88. Farm animal cutouts plus settings and animal names.
3. *Zoo Animals*, No. 90.
4. *Our Pets*, No. 92.
5. *The School*, No. 134. Cutouts of over twenty familiar objects and people found in the school.
6. *The Circus*, No. 140. Complete set of characters and circus scenery.
7. *Simple Transportation*, No. 141.
8. *Cars and Trucks*, No. 142.
9. *Trains*, No. 143.
10. *Water Transportation*, No. 144.
11. *Air Transportation*, No. 145.
12. *The Community*, No. 147.
13. *Community Helpers*, No. 150.
14. *Community Workers*, No. 151.

Science Readiness Aids for Flannel Board Use

1. *Seasons*, No. 286.
2. *Water Cycle*, No. 272.
3. *Animals in Streams and Ponds*, No. 281.
4. *Animals in the Woods*, No. 282.
5. *Animals in the Field*, No. 283.

Nutrition Lessons

1. *Nutrition*, No. 276.
2. *Balanced Meals*, No. 277.

Arithmetic Readiness

1. *Primary Cut-Outs*, No. 10.
2. *Holiday Primary Cut-Outs*, No. 25.

3. *Numerals, Words and Symbols,* No. 51.
4. *Arithmetic Readiness Vocabulary,* No. 27. "Old Woman in the Shoe" theme with different sizes of individual children, groups of children, windows, trees, to illustrate such mathematical concepts as *many, few, more, less, big, little,* etc.

Language Arts Readiness (Reading Readiness)

1. *Rhyming Pictures,* No. 32.
2. *Opposites Concepts,* No. 33.
3. *Toy Chest of Beginning Sounds,* No. 34.
4. *Classification,* No. 36.
5. *Color Recognition,* No. 55.

Creative Stories Series

Favorite Stories Series

Instructional Aids

1. *See-quees Reading Aids* for telling a story. Pictures to organize sequence and narration to shape the story. Each episode is a 3″ miniature picture that fits squarely into the inlay board background. Nursery Rhyme Series, Stories and Childhood Events, and the Nature and Science Series. Available from R. H. Stone Products, Box 414, Detroit, Michigan (48231).

2. *Stick-O-Mats.* For use with flannelboards. They can be drawn or written upon and grouped on the flannelboard. Children can work with them for special activities or other assignments. Four shapes are available-Circles, squares, triangles and rectangles. Graduated 2″, 4″, 6″, 8″.

3. *Reading Readiness Charts.* Set contains nine charts, printed in color on white tag, 23″ x 36″ with metal eyelets. Chart depicts Developing Rhyming Words, Selecting Rhyming Words, Pictures Alike—Different, Recognition of Size, Identification of Lower Case Letters, Action Pictures and Name Words. No. L599 with manual $4.00. Chart Racks Available.

4. To supplement Reading Readiness Charts: *Objects That Rhyme*—Twenty toy models of everyday objects that rhyme, such as *house-mouse,* etc., $2.50 per set.

5. *Source: Instructo Educational Toys:* No. T-400 Instructo

Fun N' Felt: A new flannel-board toy which comes complete with a 16″ x 20″ flannel board and over 125 assorted Felt cutouts including numbers, letters, birds and assorted geometric shapes. Helps pupils spell, play arithmetic and create felt pictures right on their own flannel board. Illustrated suggestion sheet included. $4.00.

6. Scott, Louise Binder: *Soundie's Magnetic Learning Board.* Magnetized flannel-like surface that permits flannel board and magnetic board activities simultaneously on a common surface, adding visual stimuli to aural-oral experiences for reading and spelling. The instructional pamphlet suggests activities for flannel board rhymes, story-telling, speech practice, social studies, etc. Available from Webster Division, McGraw-Hill Book Co., 1154 Reco Avenue, St. Louis, Missouri (63126).

7. Materials available from Ideals Publishing Co. P.O. Box 1101 Milwaukee, Wisconsin (53201)
   a. Picture Prints of Children   Set #3
   b. Children and Pets   Set #7
                                      Set #12   Price $1.00
   c. Booklets for Children: *Aesop's Fables,* and *Down Mother Goose Lane*, both 50c.

8. Safety scissors for preschool children to use are available from Nu-Dell Plastics Corporation of Chicago. They are inexpensively sold in many five-and ten-cent stores or toy departments.

9. *The Hook N' Loop Board* may be purchased from:
The Ohio Flock-Cote Company, 5713 Euclid Avenue, Cleveland, Ohio (44103).
Charles Mayer Studios, Inc., 776 Commins St., Akron 7, Ohio.
Tecnifax, 15780 Schaefer, Detroit, Michigan

10. Plastic "take-apart" figures:
Walt Disney's Snap-eeze by Marx. ©Walt Disney Productions.
Louis Marx & Co., Inc.

11. Peg Board by Judy, The Judy Company, Minneapolis, Minnesota.

Source

Associated School Distributors, Inc., 220 West Madison Street, Chicago 6, Illinois.

1. Action Pictures for Flannel Board.
2. Pegboard.
3. Peg-Flannel Board Combination.
4. *What's Missing?* Lotto.
5. *Go Together.* Lotto.
6. *World About Us.* Lotto.
7. *Farm.* Lotto.
8. *Zoo.* Lotto.
9. *Object.* Lotto.
10. *Animal.* Dominos.
11. *Picture.* Dominos.

Source: Ginn and Company, Russell, Clymer, and Christenson: *Building Pre-reading Skills.*
Sixteen 18″ x 24″ illustrations which depict fanciful stories and poems and realistic experiences.

1. Learning About the Zoo.
2. Learning About Mother and Baby Animals.
3. Distinguishing Between Real and Make Believe.
4. Telling A Story About the Zoo.
5. Learning Nursery Rhymes.

Filmstrips

Source: The Jam Handy Organization, 2821 East Grand Boulevard, Detroit 31, Michigan, and the Jam Handy Organization of Canada, Limited.

Picture Stories for Reading Readiness—Series I

1. *The Squirrels' Picnic.*
2. *Lost at the Fair*
3. *Puppy Plays A Trick.*
4. *The Loose Tooth.*
5. *Buying a Pet.*
6. *Suprise for Daddy.*
7. *Let's Go to the Zoo.*

(Complete series, $22.75.   Individual filmstrips, $3.75)

Picture Series—Series II

1. Making Christmas Cookies.

2. An Airplane Trip.
3. Fishing With Daddy.
4. A Visit to the Dentist.
5. Shopping for Groceries.
6. The New Baby.
  (Complete series $25.50.   Individual Filmstrips, $4.75.)

Old Tales for Young Folks

1. *The Three Bears.*
2. *The Three Billy Goats Gruff.*
3. *The Three Spinners.*
4. *The Sweet Porridge.*
5. *The Golden Goose.*
6. *The Three Little Pigs.*
  (Complete series, $31.50.   Individual filmstrips, $5.75.)

Tales from Grimm and Anderson

1. *The Shoemaker and the Elves.*
2. *The Wolf and the Seven Little Kids.*
3. *Rapunzel.*
4. *The Frog Prince.*
5. *Spindle, Shuttle and Needle.*
6. *Hans Clodhopper.*
7. *The Princess on the Pea.*
  (Complete series, $36.75.   Individual filmstrips, $5.75.)

Growing Things

1. Plants Grow.
2. Trees Grow.
3. Butterflies Grow.
4. Toads Grow.
5. Birds Grow.
6. Rabbits Grow.
7. We Grow.
  (Complete series, $36.75.   Individual filmstrips, $5.75.)

The Farmer's Animal Friends

1. Cows on the Farm.

2. Horses on the Farm.
3. Pigs on the Farm.
4. Sheep on the Farm.
5. Chickens on the Farm.
6. Cats on the Farm.
(Complete series, $31.50.   Individual filmstrips, $5.75.)

Animal Stories

1. Rings, the Raccoon.
2. The Lazy Bear Cub.
3. Brush, the Red Squirrel.
4. Mrs. Cackles Becomes A Good Citizen.
5. Hoppy the Rabbit.
6. The Adventure of Pete and His Dog.
(Complete series, $31.50.
Individual filmstrips, $5.75.)
Filmstrips available from:
  Eye-Gate House, Inc.
  146-01 Archer Avenue
  Jamaica 35, New York

Readiness Instructional Filmstrips

85A Recognition Phases
       Memory Span
       Color Recognition
       Vocabulary for Speaking
       Context Clues
85B Auditory Discrimination
85C Story Practices
       Following Sequences of Story
       Developing Listening Skills
       Using Narrative Expression
       Relationships and Noting Details
85D Visual Discrimination
85E Classifying
85F Similarities
85G Differences
85H Alphabet

85I Left-to-right Sequence
85J Stories for Special Days
150 Series—*Picture Stories for Reading Readiness*
166 Series—*Primary Concepts*

Source: Association of American Railroads. Color filmstrip available, *Tommy Takes A Train Trip*. Discussion leaflet included. May be obtained permanently by the school or library.

Source for Free Filmstrips

Educators' Guide to Free Filmstrips. 17th Annual Edition, 1965. Educators' Progress Service, Randolph, Wisconsin.

Filmstrips from: Encyclopedia Britannica Films, Inc., 1150 Wilmette Avenue, Wilmette, Illinois (60091).

Reading Readiness Series (Color)

1. Going Places.
2. Going Downtown.
3. Going to the Country.
4. Going to the Zoo.
5. Roy's Toys.
6. All Kinds of Houses.
7. What's Wrong?
8. Playing Community Helpers.
9. Going Shopping.

Shortstrips—Designed for individual pupil viewing with a hand or desk viewer. Can also be projected on a screen.
Shortstrips recommended for readiness:

Learning About Animals, Series No. 9940 (Color). Each shortstrip contains fourteen frames.

1. My Dog Sandy.
2. Playful Kittens
3. Cows on the Farm.
4. Prince the Riding Horse.
5. Pigs on the Farm.
6. The Wooly Sheep.
7. A Great Family.
8. Mother Duck and Her Friends.
9. Chickens on the Farm.
10. Mother Rabbit and Her Family.

11. Mother Gray Squirrel.

12. Let's Look at Birds.

Order from: John Martin Kroll, Teaching Filmstrips, 1508 N. Sheridan Road, Waukegan, Illinois.

Filmstrips with narration records from: Storytoons, Inc., 735 Fairfield Avenue, Kenilworth, New Jersey.

127 The Dog and His Shadow.

117 The Elves and the Shoemaker.

113 The Gingerbread Boy.

119 Little Red Riding Hood.

134 Mother Goose Rhymes Group 1

122 Mother Goose Rhymes Group 2

106 Musicians of Bremen.

112 The Owl and the Pussy Cat and My Shadow.

110 The Princess and the Pea.

121 Sleeping Beauty.

129 The Table and the Chair.

107 Three Billy Goats Gruff.

135 The Wind and the Sun.

Society for Visual Education, Inc. 1345 Diversey Parkway Chicago 14, Illinois.

These series are recommended especially for readiness:

Wild Animals.

Common Birds

Pets and Farm and Ranch Animals

Learning About the Seasons Series.

Familiar Animals and Their Families Series.

Animal Friends (Story series with Records to accompany).

Elf Book Filmstrip Series Group 1 stories.

Children's Classics Series of Stories.

Hans Christian Andersen Fairy Tales.

Children's Fairy Tales.

Holidays—Easter, and Springtime, Thanksgiving, Christmas Holiday Series.

Picture Dictionaries

1. Eastman, P.D.: The cat in the hat. *Beginner Book Dictionary,* Random House, Inc., 1964.

2. McIntire, Alta; *Picture Dictionary.* Chicago, Follett Publishing Co., 1959.
3. MacBean, Dilla: *Picture Book Dictionary* with a Picture Story. Chicago, Children's Press, 1952, 1962. $2.50.
4. Oftedal, Laura and Jacob, Nina: *My First Dictionary.* New York, Grosset and Dunlap, 1948.

Instructional Aids Recommended for Use by Parents

1. Highlights Handbook: *Getting Ready to Read,* by Dr. and Mrs. Garry Cleveland Myers. Highlights for Children, Inc. Columbus, Ohio, 1958.
2. "Ready or Not?" The School Readiness Checklist, by John J. Austin and J. Clayton Lafferty. Research Concepts, 36176 Parkdale, Livonia, Michigan 1963.
3. *Finger Plays and Action Rhymes,* by Frances E. Jacobs. Lothrop, Lee and Shepard Co., 1941.
4. *Homes,* by Virginia Parsons. 1958 Copyright by Doubleday Co., Inc.
   Night, by Virginia Parsons. 1958 Published by Garden City Books.
5. *Rain,* by Virginia Parsons. Garden City, 1961 Doubleday and Company, Inc.
6. *The Wonder Book of Counting Rhymes,* by June Pierce. New York, Wonder Books. A division of Grosset and Dunlap, Inc., 1957. Price 29c.
7. Wright Betty Ren: *I Want to Read!* Racine, Whitman Publishing Co., 1965.

Inexpensive Materials Available at Stores

1. *Animal Rummy Card Game,* Whitman Publishing Company.
2. *Hearts Card Game,* E. E. Fairchild Corporation Rochester, New York.
   Crazy Faces Card Game, (Picture cards for use with matching, indicating likenesses and differences, etc.).
3. *What Does It Eat?,* Saalfield Artcraft, (Animal and food pictures for matching.).
4. *Where Does It Belong?,* (Pictured items for matching those that are used together, such as door and key, etc.).

5. *Picture Words for Beginners,* Milton Bradley Co. Springfield, Massachusetts.
6. *Picture Readiness Game,* by E. W. Dolch, PhD., University of Illinois.
7. Dennison lettersets   (15c)
   Dennison Stars   (15c)
   Dennison Manufacturing Co. Framingham, Massachusetts (For use with matching likenesses, differences, counting, color matching and recognition, etc.)
8. *Build with Stencils,* (Using simple shapes and colored paper. Matching shapes according to likenesses.).
   Whitman Publishing Co. Racine, Wisconsin (c. 1964), 29c.
9. Nut cups, plastic spoons, baking cups, wooden spoons, forks, etc. may be purchased for preparation of materials for matching. Many other inexpensive materials may be obtained at five-and-ten cent stores.

Children's Books

1. Bradfield, Joan and Roger: *The Big Happy A B C.* Racine, Whitman Publishing Company, 1965, $1.00.
2. Bradfield, Joan and Roger: *The Big Happy 1 2 3.* Racine, Whitman Publishing Company, 1965, $1.00.
3. Bradfield Roger: *There's An Elephant in the Bathtub.* Racine, Whitman Publishing Co., 1964.
4. Brown, Palmer: *Something for Christmas.* New York, Harper & Row Publishers, 1958, $1.95.
5. Conkling, Fleur, *The Bingity-Bangity School Bus.* New York, Wonder Books, Inc., 1950, 29c.
6. Daugherty, Charles M.: *Wisher.* New York, The Viking Press, 1960.
7. Dolch, Edward W., and Margaret P.: *Big, Bigger, Biggest.* Champaign, Garrard Publishing Co., 1959.
8. Dolch, Edward W., and Marguerite P.: *Zoo Is Home.* Champaign, Garrard Publishing Co., 1958.
9. Hogan, Inez: *Nicodemus and the Gang.* New York, E. P. Dutton, 1939, 1943, 1953. (Others are included in this series.).
10. Konkle, Janet: *The Christmas Kitten.* Chicago, Children's Press, 1953.

11. MacDonald, Golden: *Red Light, Green Light.* Garden City, Doubleday, 1944.
12. Pratt, Marjorie, and Meighen, Mary: *Fun For You.* Chicago, Benj. H. Sanborn, and Co., 1956.
13. Seuss, Dr., *Green Eggs and Ham.* New York, Beginner Books, and Toronto, Random House of Canada, 1960. (Also *Hop on Pop* and the other delightful Seuss Books.)
14. Shane, Harold G., and Hester, Kathleen B., *Tales to Read.* Laidlow Brothers River Forest, Illinois, Summit, N. J., Palo Alto, Calif., Dallas, Atlanta, 1961.
15. Skaar, Grace: *The Little Red House,* Eau Claire, E. M. Hale and Company, 1955.
16. Weil, Ann and Vernam, Roger: *Animal Families.* Chicago, Children's Press, 1956.

Song Books

1. *50 Songs for Children,* by Mary Nancy Graham. Racine, Whitman Publishing Co., 1964. 29c.
2. *The Magic of Music, Book One,* by Lorrain E. Watters, Louise Wersen, William Hartshorn, L. Eileen McMillan, Alice Gallup and Frederick Beckman. Boston Ginn and Company. 1965.

Records

1. Rhythm Record for Primary Children Reading and Number Readiness. Available from Rhythm Record Co. 9203 Nichols Rd. Oklahoma City, Oklahoma.
   Distributed by F. A. Owen Publishing Co. Dansville, New York.
2. The Kiddie Korner long-playing children's records. Distributed by Sapien Enterprises, 16500 Main Street, Gardena, California.

SELECTED BIBLIOGRAPHY

Suggested by the Curriculum Research Committee* for Classroom Action Research Projects

I. *Background and Overview of the Research Process*
  A. General Considerations

  COREY, STEPHEN N.: *Action Research to Improve School Practices.* New York, Teachers College, Columbia University, 1953.

  TRAVERS, ROBERTS M.: *An Introduction to Educational Research.* New York, The MacMillan Co., 1958.

  VANDALEN, DEOBALD D.: *Understanding Educational Research.* New York, McGraw-Hill, 1962.

  B. Special Problem Areas

  BARNES, JOHN B.: *Educational Research for Classroom Teachers.* New York, Putnam; 1960.

  TORGETSON, THEODORE L.: *Measurement and Evaluation for the Elementary School Teacher.* New York, The Dryden Press, 1954.

II. *Design of Research (Especially Experimental Research)*
  A. General Considerations

  SELLTIZ, C., JAHODA, M., DEUTSCH, M., and COOK, S.W.: *Research Methods in Social Relations.* New York, Holt, Rinehart and Winston, 1959.

III. *Sampling Procedures*
  A. General Considerations

  PARTEN, M. B.: *Surveys, Polls, and Samples: Practical Procedures.* New York, Harper and Brothers 1950.

IV. *Data Collection*
  A. General Considerations

  REMMERS, H. H., GAGE, N. L., and RUMMEL, J. F.: *A Practical Introduction to Measurement and Evaluation.* New York, Harper Brothers, 1960.

---

*Curriculum Research Committee, *Ibid,* pp. 17-18. (This is a portion of the selected bibliography suggested in *Solving Classroom Problems Through Systematic Study.*)

B. Special Problem Areas

PAYNE, S. L.: *The Art of Asking Questions*. Princeton, Princeton University Press, 1951.

FURST, E. J.: *Constructing Evaluation Instruments*. New York, Longmans, Green and Co., 1958.

REMMERS, H. H.: *Introduction to Opinion and Attitude Measurement*. New York, Harper and Brothers, 1954.

Tests and Measurement Kit. Princeton, Educational Testing Service.

No. 1 Locating Information on Educational Measurement:
Sources and References 1965

No. 3 Selecting An Achievement Test:
Principles and Procedures 1958, 1961

No. 4 Making the Classroom Test:
A Guide for Teachers 1959, 1961

No. 5 Short-Cut Statistics for Teacher-Made Tests 1960, 1964
Multiple-Choice Questions: A Close Look 1963
ETS Builds A Test 1959, 1965
Testing Programs
Special Services
Instructional Activities at Educational Testing
Service 1966

V. *Data Analysis (Logic of Analytic and Statistical Procedures)*

A. General Considerations

MORONEY, M. J.: *Facts From Figures*. London, Penguin Books, 1958.

VI. *Statistical Methods*

A. Special Problem Areas

SIEGEL, SIDNEY: *Nonparametric Statistics for the Sciences*. New York, McGraw-Hill, 1956.

BIBLIOGRAPHY

1, ASBELL, BERNARD: Six years old is too late. *Redbook,* September, 1965, Vol. 125, No. 5, pp. 53, 124-8.
2. AUSTIN, MARY C., and MORRISON, COLEMAN: "The First R: The Harvard Report on Reading in Elementary Schools." New York, The Macmillan Company, 1963.
3. BAUMGARTNER, BERNICE B.: *Helping the Trainable Mentally Retarded Child,* New York, Bureau of Publications, Teachers College Columbia University, 1960.
4. BOND, GUY L., and TINKER, MILES A.: *Reading Difficulties: Their Diagnosis and Correction.* New York, Appleton-Century-Crofts, 1957.
5. BRUNNER, CATHERINE: More than an ounce of prevention. *Childhood Education.* September, 1965, Vol. 42, No. 1 pp. 35-43.
6. BURTON, WILLIAM H.: *Reading in Child Development.* New York, Bobbs-Merrill Co., 1956.
7. CLYMER, THEODORE, CHRISTENSON, BERNICE M., and RUSSELL, DAVID H.: *Manual for Building Pre-reading Skills, Kit A, Language.* Boston, Ginn and Company, 1965.
8. CLYMER, THEODORE, CHRISTENSON, BERNICE M., and RUSSELL, DAVID H.: *Manual for Building Pre-reading Skills, Kit B.* Boston, Ginn and Company, 1965.
9. DALE, EDGAR: *Audiovisual Methods in Teaching,* Revised Edition. New York, Holt, Rinehart and Winston, 1954.
10. DELP, HAROLD A.: The 3 I's, not the 3 R's: a philosophy for teachers of mentally retarded. *The Training School Bulletin,* May, 1958, Vol. 55, No. 1, pp. 11-14.
11. DURBIN, MARY LOU: Peg board drills for the trainable. *The Pointer for Special Class Teachers and Parents of the Handicapped,* Vol. 10, No. 2, 1966, pp. 55-6. The Association for Special Class Teachers and Parents of the Handicapped, Inc. Grass Valley, California.
12. DURBIN, MARY LOU, and KAYE, CLEMENT L.: Materials and the severely retarded. *The Michigan Education Journal.* March 1, 1963, Vol. XL, No. 14, pp. 501, 526.
13. D'EVELYN, KATHERINE: Meeting Children's Emotional Needs: *A Guide for Teachers.* Englewood Cliffs, Prentice-Hall, Inc., 1957.

14. ENGELBERG, MORTON R.: The other America. *The Michigan Education Journal.* March, 1965, Vol. 42, pp. 9-10.
15. HAUBRICH, VERNON F.: The Culturally Disadvantaged and Teacher Education. *The Reading Teacher,* March, 1965, Vol. 18, No. 6, pp. 502-3. The International Reading Association Newark, Delaware.
16. HESTER, KATHLEEN B.: *Teaching Every Child to Read.* New York, Harper & Row, 1948 and 1955.
17. HOGGARD, KENDALL J.: Readiness is the best prevention. *Readings on Reading Instruction,* Edited by Albert J. Harris. New York, David McKay Company, 1963.
    Originally printed in *Education,* LXXVII, May, 1957.

18. HOUSE, BETTY L., and ZEAMAN, DAVID: Visual discrimination learning and intelligence in defectives of low mental age. *The American Journal of Mental Deficiency,* July, 1960, Vol. 65, pp. 51-8.
    The American Association on Mental Deficiency, 401 South Spring Street Springfield, Illinois (62706).
19. HURLOCK, ELIZABETH B.: *Child Growth and Development.* New York, McGraw-Hill, 1956.
20. HYMES, JAMES L., JR.: *Behavior and Misbehavior.* Englewood Cliffs, Prentice-Hall, 1955.
21. JOHNSON, ORVILLE G.: *Education For The Slow Learners.* Englewood Cliffs, Prentice-Hall, 1963.
22. JOHNSON, SAMUEL and ORVILLE: *Educating The Retarded Child.* Boston, Houghton Mifflin, 1951.
23. KIRK, SAMUEL, WINFORD, KIRK, and KARNES, MERLE: *You and Your Retarded Child.* New York, Macmillan, 1955.
24. KIRK, SAMUEL, and STEVENS, IRENE: A pre-academic curriculum for slow-learning children. *The American Journal of Mental Deficiency,* Vol. 47, No. 4, April, 1942, pp. 396-413.
25. LANGDON, GRACE, and STOUT, IRVING W.: *Teaching in the Primary Grades.* New York, Macmillan, 1964.
26. LEVINE, DANIEL U.: City schools today: too late with too little. *Phi Delta Kappan* November, 1962, pp. 82-3.
27. LLOYD, HELENE M.: What's ahead in reading for the disadvantaged? *The Reading Teacher.* March, 1965, Vol. 18, No. 6, pp. 471-2
28. Maplewood Parent-Teachers Association: *Community Classroom.* Maplewood School, Garden City, Michigan, 1963.

29. MERGENTIME, CHARLOTTE: *You and Your Child's Reading*. New York, Harcourt, Brace and World, 1963.

30. MICHIGAN EDUCATION JOURNAL: Project Head Start. From "What's Ahead for Michigan?" May, 1965, Vol. 42, No. 19, p. 65.

31. McPHERSON, MARION WHITE: Learning and mental deficiency. *The American Journal of Mental Deficiency,* March, 1958, Vol. 62, No. 5, pp. 870-877.

32. NEWTON, JOHN ROY: *Reading in Your School*. New York, Mc-Graw-Hill, 1960.

33. OLSEN, JAMES: Challenge of the poor to the schools. *Phi Delta Kappan,* October, 1965, pp. 79-84.

34. ROSENZWEIG, LOUIS: How far have we come? *Amercian Journal of Mental Deficiency.* July 1959. Vol. 64, No. 1, p. 13.

35. SHANE, HAROLD G., MULRY, JUNE, REDDIN, MARY E., and GILLESPIE, MARGARET C.: Improving Language Arts Instruction in the Elementary School, Columbus, Charles E. Merrill Books, 1962.

36. SHAW, JULES HAROLD: Vision and seeing skills of preschool children. *The Reading Teacher.* October, 1964, Vol. 18, No. 1, pp. 35-6.

37. SHELLEY, ARDITH: My Jack-o-lantern. *The Ginn Music News.* Fall, 1964, Ginn and Company.

38. SMITH, MARIAN: *Teaching the Slow Learning Child*. New York, Harper & Row, 1954.

39. STROM, ROBERT D.: *Teaching in the Slum School*. Columbus, Charles E. Merrill, 1965.

40. WARGO, GERALD J.: Physical education and recreation for mentally retarded children. *The Physical Educator.* May, 1961, Vol. 18, No. 2, pp. 65-6. Phi Epsilon Kappa Fraternity, 3747 North Linwood Avenue, Indianapolis, Indiana (46218).

41. WATTERS, LORRAIN E., WERSEN, LOUIS, HARTSHORN, WILLIAM, McMILLIAN, L. EILEEN, and GALLUP, ALICE: *The Magic of Music,* Book 1. Boston, Ginn and Company, 1965.

42. WILES, KIMBALL: *Teaching for Better Schools*. Englewood Cliffs, Prentice-Hall, 1952.

43. WILLIAMS, HAROLD M.: *Education of the Severely Retarded Child, OE-35022*. Bulletin, 1961, No. 20. U.S. Department of Health, Education and Welfare, Office of Education.

NAME INDEX

Appalachia, 149
Asbell, Bernard, 159, 160
Austin, Mary C., 90

Baltimore Public Schools, 149, 157
Baumgartner, Bernice B., 93, 94
Bond, Guy L., 130, 131, 181, 218
Boston, Massachusetts, 147
Brunner, Catherine, 149, 157
Burton, William H., 35, 36

Christenson, Bernice M., 37, 38, 54, 55, 56, 61
Clymer, Theodore, 37, 38, 54, 55, 56, 61
Columbia University, 151
Committee on Human Development, 160
Courville School, 173
Curriculum Research Committee, 216, 243

Dale, Edgar, 181, 182, 189
Delp, Harold, PhD., 212
Department of Curriculum and Teaching, 150
Detroit, Michigan, 149
Detroit, Michigan Public Schools, 151, 152, 158, 173
Durbin, Mary Lou, 128, 179, 192, 210, 213
D'Evelyn, Katherine, 33

Early School Admission Project, 149
Economic Opportunity Act of 1964, The, 149, 150
Engelberg, Morton R., 150
Everett, Edward, 10

F. A. Owen Publishing Company, 64
Farrell, Alta, 158, 159, 173, 174
Ford Foundation, 157

Gallup, Alice, 64
Garden City, Michigan, 9, 67, 158, 186
Germany, 158
Gillespie, Margaret C., 42, 48, 65, 180
Great City School Improvement Program, 152

Harlem, 149, 150
Harris, Albert J., 217
Hartshorn, William L., 64
Hasting Street, 149
Haubrich, Vernon F., 150, 151
Hess, Robert, Dr., 160
Hester, Kathleen B., 205
Hoggard Kendall J., 217
House, Betty L., 214
Hunter College, 150, 151
Hurlock, Elizabeth B., 132, 133, 134
Hymes, James L., Jr., 33

Ideal School Supply Co., 96

Job Corps, The, 149, 150
Johnson, Orville G., 20, 220
Johnson, Roberta, 56, 57
Johnson, Samuel, 20

Karnes, Merle, 10, 17
Kaye, Clement L., 213
Kirk, Samuel, 10, 17, 21
Kirk, Winford, 10, 17

249

SUBJECT INDEX

A

Ability, assessment of mental, 17; auditory, 37; decision-making, 163; lack of, 91; leadership, 24; listening and observing, 65; mental, 11; of trainable, 128; to learn, 9, 36; to scrutinize, 208; verbal, 21; visual acuity, 37

Abstract, interpretation of, 182, learning, 180

Achievement, adequate pupil, 20

Actions, words to describe, 41

Activities, class, 34, 187; classification, 176, 177; concept-building, 165, 166, 167, 168, 169, 170, 171, 172, 173; 174, 175, 176, 177, 178, 179; culminating, 135, 203; cutting and pasting, 43; developmental, 202; discussion, 61, 204; easy and challenging, 20; enrichment, 180, 183; family life, 132; finger play, 123; follow-up, 46; for skill development, 93; handicraft, 123, 162; independent, 86, 89, 90, 178; interesting, 53; introductory, 202; listening, 68, 164; manipulative, 144, 221, 222; matching, 5; meaningful, 41, 139; music, 123; parental help with, 35; poems, 123; prereading, 40; science, 122; seatwork, 51, 120, 168, 178; small group, 179; structured, 27; summer school 143; supervised, 89; supplementary, 20, 51, 120, 165, 166, 167, 183, 184, 208; testing, 222; to overcome effects of crowded living, 163; trainable child's seatwork, 96; varied, 183, 190; workbook, 51

Adjustment, emotional, 35; social, 10, 14, 15, 35

Aesthetic, appreciation, 127; needs, 38

Agencies, outside the school, 19

Aids for testing and diagnosis, 183; visual, 183.
See also Audiovisual Aids.

Animals, classification, 43; in science, 122, 125; pets, 125, 153, 154; recognition of, 164; sounds of, 203; zoo and farm, 125, 174, 189

Areas, of difficulty, 78

Art, activities, 162; appreciation, 180

Association, of related pictures, 137; of related things 137, 189, 205; of words and meanings, 138, 227; skills, 138

Attention, ability, 139; capturing materials 186; span, 5, 50, 51, 61, 116, 144, 219, 221; trainable child's span of, 95

Attitudes, favorable for reading, 35, 37, 183; general teacher, 34; of disadvantaged, 157, 158; of mother upon learning patterns, 160; of retarded, 21; of trainable, 123; pupil self-respect and confidence 18

Audiologist, 37

Auditory, abilities, 37, disabilities, 29, discrimination, 39, 48, 138, 139, 179, 203, 226; handicaps, 212; perception, 37, 56; perception skills, 55; readiness, 46; skill instruction, 47; skills, 30, 131

Audiovisual

Aids, balanced use of, 182; for science, 123; goals of program, 186; in readiness, 40, 161, 164, 180, 182; in teaching, 180, 183; in testing, 222; interrelationships of, 181; need for, 183; preparation of, 185; role in readiness, 188, 200; scope of the program, 186; tools for reinforcement, 182; used in classification, 177; wise use of, 183, 209, 210

committees, 186; coordinator, 185, 186, 187; county center, 187, 221; director, 186, 187

equipment, 52, 128, 152, 186, 187, 209; delineascope, 199, 200; flannel board, 51, 53, 59, 63, 116, 172, 176, 189, 190, 191, 192, 193, 194, 196; Hook N' Loop Board, 63, 189, 191, 192, 194, 198, 199, 203, 204, 234; magnetic board, 208, pegboard, 51, 191, 192, 193, 194, 208; projectors,

251